Feast of St Monica, 2008.

FREEDOM AND NECESSITY

FREEDOM
AND
NECESSITY

St. Augustine's Teaching on Divine Power and Human Freedom

GERALD BONNER

The Catholic University of America Press
Washington, D.C.

The paper used in this publication meets the minimum requirements of American National Standards for Information Science—Permanence of Paper for Printed Library Materials, ANSI Z39.48-1984.

∞

Library of Congress Cataloging-in-Publication Data
Bonner, Gerald.
Freedom and necessity : St. Augustine's teaching on divine power and human freedom / Gerald Bonner.
p. cm.
Includes bibliographical references and index.
ISBN-13: 978-0-8132-1474-0 (pbk. : alk. paper)
ISBN-10: 0-8132-1474-2 (pbk. : alk. paper) 1. Augustine, Saint, Bishop of Hippo. 2. Grace (Theology)—History of doctrines—Early church, ca. 30–600. 3. Free will and determinism—Religious aspects—Christianity—History of doctrines—Early church, ca. 30–600. 4. Predestination—History of doctrines—Early church, ca. 30–600. I. Title.
BR65.A9B626 2006
234′.9092—dc22
2006019364

The author's English spelling has been altered by the Catholic University of America Press without reference to him, to conform to its own norms.

To all my fellow-students over the years

and especially to Jane

CONTENTS

PREFATORY NOTE

THE PURPOSE OF THIS WORK is to set out, as fairly as I can, Augustine's final understanding of divine predestination and his attempt to reconcile it with his continued assertion that free choice continues to exist in fallen human beings. I also wish to make clear how grim are the conclusions which he draws from his doctrine of Original Sin, which to me seem irreconcilable with the Gospel message, but which are supported by texts of Scripture, including some words of Christ Himself, and which have been accepted by generations of Christians, who were not themselves lacking in sympathy and charity for other human beings. At the same time, I have attempted to remind the reader that Augustine's thinking is not simply negative. Many years ago, in a study of Augustine's theology, I remarked that "it would be possible, though it would require careful selection, to read widely in Augustine without ever considering his doctrine of Grace."[1] When considering Augustine's eucharistic theology, his emphasis on love as the supreme virtue, and on the significance of the Word's flesh-taking in the Incarnation for God's dealings with humanity, one encounters a mood which might, in other circumstances, have led Augustine to greater hopes for the future of humanity than are found in the *De Dono Perseverantiae* and the (mercifully uncompleted) *Opus Imperfectum contra Iulianum.* Without subscribing to his thesis, I have much sympathy with Dr. P.-M. Hombert, *Gloria Gratiae: Se glorifier en Dieu, principe et fin de la théologie augustinienne de la grâce.*

For similar reasons I have found myself convinced that the Pelagians, to whom I am not naturally drawn, deserve more sympathy

1. *St. Augustine of Hippo: Life and Controversies,* 3rd ed. (2002), 389.

than they have generally received down the ages. It seems to me that their major error—an overestimation of human ability after the Fall—stemmed from zeal in urging the duty of right living in all those who claimed to be Christians. It was their misfortune that circumstances brought them into conflict with Augustine and the African episcopate which was not, I am persuaded, far behind its most distinguished spokesman in its defense of what it deemed the faith of the universal Church.

I am conscious of a debt to two authors, neither of whom is widely read today: J. K. Mozley and Thomas Allin. I first read Allin more than fifty years ago, and found his vehemence little to my taste. Now, I am inclined to agree with Sir Walter Raleigh (admittedly in very different circumstances), "So the heart be right it is no matter where the head lieth." Allin's exuberance sprang from a genuine Christian conviction. I find Mozley's judicious balance very congenial. In moments of fantasy, I wish that he and Allin could have written a book on Augustine together.

Finally, although never mentioned in the text, I would record my gratitude to the writings of the eccentric Christian convert Simone Weil. Although by Augustine's theology she is damned, being unbaptized, it seems to me that she fully understood his doctrine of grace: "Reniement de saint Pierre. Dire au Christ: je te resterai fidèle, c'était déjà le renier, car c'était supposer en soi et non dans la grâce, la source de la fidélité. Heureusement, comme il était élu, ce reniement est devenue manifeste pour tous et pour lui. Chez combien d'autres de telles vantardises s'accomplissent—et ils ne comprennent jamais."

I am grateful to Beth Benevides and to Ellen Coughlin for their help in preparing this text for publication.

ABBREVIATIONS AND SOURCES

CCL	*Corpus Christianorum Latinorum*
CSEL	*Corpus Scriptorum Ecclesiasticorum Latinorum*
PL	*Patrologia Latina*
PLS	*Patrologia Latina: Supplementum*
an. et or.	*De Anima et Origine* (*CSEL* 60)
bapt.	*De Baptismo* (*CSEL* 51)
beata v.	*De Beata Vita* (*CSEL* 63)
cat rud.	*De Catechizandis Rudibus* (*CCL* 46)
civ.	*De Civitate Dei* (*CCL* 47–48; *CSEL* 40)
conf.	*Confessionum Libri XIII* (*CCL* 27; *CSEL* 33)
cor. et grat.	*De Correptione et Gratia* (*PL* 44)
div. quaest. LXXXIII	*De diversis Quaestionibus octoginta-tribus* (*CCL* 44A)
dono pers.	*De dono Perseverantiae* (*PL* 45)
c. duas epp. Pel.	*Contra duas epistulas Pelagianorum* (*CSEL* 60)
ench.	*Enchiridion ad Laurentium* (*CCL* 46)
ep., epp.	*Epistula, Epistulae* (*CSEL* 34; 44; 57; 58; 88)
ep. Gal. exp.	*Epistulae ad Galatos expositio* (*CSEL* 84)
ep. Ioh. tr.	*In Epistulam Iohannis ad Parthos Tractatus* (*PL* 35)
exp. Rom.	*Epistulae ad Romanos inchoata expositio* (*CSEL* 84)

fid. et op.	*De Fide et Operibus* (*CSEL* 41)
gest. Pel.	*De Gestis Pelagii* (*CSEL* 42)
Gn. litt.	*De Genesi ad Litteram* (*CSEL* 28.1)
grat. Christ. et pecc. orig.	*De Gratia Christi et Peccato Originali* (*CSEL* 42)
grat. et lib. arb.	*De Gratia et Libero Arbitrio* (*PL* 44)
Ioh. ev. tr.	*In Evangelium Iohannis Tractatus* (*CCL* 36)
c. Iul.	*Contra Iulianum* (*PL* 44)
lib. arb.	*De Libero Arbitrio* (*CCL* 29; *CSEL* 74)
nat. bon.	*De Natura Boni* (*CSEL* 25.2)
nat. et grat.	*De Natura et Gratia* (*CSEL* 60)
op. imp.	*Opus Imperfectum contra Iulianum* (*CSEL* 85; *PL* 45)
ord.	*De Ordine* (*CCL* 29; *CSEL* 63)
pecc. mer. et rem.	*De Peccatorum Meritis et Remissione* (*CSEL* 60)
perf. iust. Hom.	*De Perfectione Iustitiae Hominis* (*CSEL* 42)
praed. sanct.	*De Praedestinatione Sanctorum* (*PL* 44)
en. Ps.	*Enarrationes in Psalmos* (*CCL* 38–40)
quant. an.	*De Quantitate Animae* (*CSEL* 89)
retr.	*Retractationes* (*CCL* 57; *CSEL* 36)
serm.	*Sermones* (*CCL* 41 [1–50]; *PL* 38; 39; *PLS* 2)
ad Simp.	*Ad Simplicianum* (*CCL* 44)
sp. et. litt.	*De Spiritu et Littera* (*CSEL* 60).
trin.	*De Trinitate Libri XV* (*CCL* 50; 50A)
vera relig.	*De Vera Religione* (*CCL* 32; *CSEL* 77)

FREEDOM AND NECESSITY

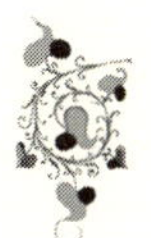

INTRODUCTION

THIS BOOK GREW OUT of a course of four lectures which I was due to give at the University of Malta in 2001. My intention was once more to examine the predestinarian theology which Augustine expressed and defended in the course of the Pelagian Controversy, and to consider how valid is his repeated claim, which was forced upon him by a succession of texts from Scripture,[1] that fallen man had, nevertheless, under the influence of grace, the opportunity to exercise free choice, and so to be a responsible agent. Against this I sought to suggest that the Pelagians, an amorphous group of theologians who have been much abused over the centuries as archheretics who denied the need for efficacious grace, did in fact defend the human responsibility which Augustine seemed, in practice, to deny, while at the same time justifying the damnation of the greater part of the human race for the inherited guilt of Adam's primal sin. The reason for raising yet again the topic of Augustinian predeterminism was the influence which it has exercised on Western Christian theology, and not simply Protestant theology, down the ages.

In the event, illness prevented me from delivering the lectures, and the preparation of a short historical commentary on the monastic rules of Augustine constrained me for two years to delay thought of possible publication. In the meantime I decided that in trying to evaluate Augustine's thinking on predestination and free will, it was desirable to consider his thought on other theological topics, both before and during the

1. See *De Gratia et Libero Arbitrio*, passim. *PL* 44,881–912.

steady stream of his predestinarian writings between 411 and his death in 430, in order to avoid the easily acquired impression that, during that period, he had no interest other than anti-Pelagian writing. The composition of the *Retractations* in 426/7 and the *De Haeresibus* in 428/9, while at the same time working on the *Opus Imperfectum* against Julian, easily demolishes that impression. Augustine was all his life prepared to write on each and any theological topic which might be presented to him; but he remained determined to defend his views on the issues raised by the Pelagians in all their rigor. He would concede that unbaptized infants might suffer the mildest torments in hell and that their state might be preferable to non-existence; but he continued to maintain the damnation of the overwhelming majority of the human race for lack of the sacrament of baptism, while insisting that the Christian God was a God of Love.

It is generally agreed among scholars that the theological views asserted by Augustine against Pelagius and his supporters were initially formed in his answers to the questions of Simplicianus of Milan in 396/7. Augustine himself certainly considered this to be the case, as witness his comment on the *Ad Simplicianum* in the *Retractations:* "In the solution of this question [Gn. 25:23; Rom. 9:11] I labored in defense of the free choice of the human will, but the grace of God conquered." What Augustine says here, in respect of Genesis 25:23 *(Two nations are in your womb . . .),* can be applied to his anti-Manichaean writings as a whole, from his conversion until writing to Simplicianus. He had initially been concerned to defend human free choice against Manichaean determinism. Against the dualism of the Manichees he maintained God's absolute supremacy over His creation, and against their assertion that men sinned because of their evil material nature, he continued to assert that sin was a moral failing, which arose from misuse of free will. Over the years, however, under the influence of St. Paul, divine omnipotence came increasingly to dominate his mind, and in writing to Simplicianus, perhaps under the influence of St. Cyprian, the significance of 1 Corinthians 4:7: *"What have you that you did not receive? And if you received it, why do you boast, as if it were not a gift?"* overwhelmed him, and from then onwards the absolute power of God, the creator of the world from nothing, dominated his thinking. The essence of sin, both angelic and human, is pride—the desire of a created being to set itself up in opposition to its Creator. By this sin fell the angels, and by it Adam, and in him fell the whole of humanity. The Pelagian assertion of free will seemed to Augustine a denial of the need of divine grace.

Clearly, this was unfair to the Pelagians; and we are faced with the problem: why did Augustine react with such sustained violence and bitterness against a movement which neither denied the Catholic Creed, as did Manichaeism; nor preached separation, as did Donatism; nor denied the divinity of the Son, as did Arianism?

One factor must have dominated: the belief that the Pelagians asserted a human independence of God, which left no need for efficacious grace. This comes out strongly in Augustine's treatise *De Gratia Christi et de Peccato Originali,* written to Pelagius's patrons Albina, Melania, and Pinianus, after his condemnation in 418, when Pelagius protested his orthodoxy, maintaining that the grace of Christ was necessary, not only for every hour or moment, but for every individual action of our lives. Augustine replied that he had never found any satisfactory recognition of the nature of grace in Pelagius's writings and refused to accept this declaration of faith.[2] Behind this rejection may be seen Augustine's concern to defend the doctrine of Original Sin *as he himself interpreted it.* Some Pelagians, like Rufinus of Syria and Caelestius, did in fact reject the doctrine; but Pelagius, while reporting their rejection, did not either associate himself with it nor specifically reject it. There may well have been an element of caution in Pelagius, which caused him not to go too deeply into questions which he regarded as not having been authoritatively defined; but Augustine was now determined to impose on the Church his own understanding of the nature and effect of Original Sin on humanity, and of the necessity of baptism for the salvation of all ages of fallen humanity.

2. *Grat. Christ. et pecc. orig.* 1,35,38. *CSEL* 42,154.

What reason lay behind this inflexibility? One may assume a genuine conviction of the rightness of his understanding of the doctrine, which commanded the enthusiastic support of Augustine's African colleagues, ever persuaded that the faith of Africa was the faith of Catholic Christians the world over. It had not been without reason that Augustine, in his sermon 294 in the Basilica Maiorum at Carthage on 27 June 413,[3] had appealed to Cyprian's letter 64 to defend the practice of infant baptism, to free children from the infection of the ancient death drawn from their birth, and to secure remission of "alien sins not their own."[4] For Augustine, Original Sin had become so much a part of his understanding of Christian theology that he regarded it as a universal article of faith.

But there may have been more personal factors in Augustine's motives in pressing the anti-Pelagian cause. Julian of Eclanum sarcastically referred to him as the "Punic Aristotle."[5] Such rudeness was, of course, a commonplace in pamphlet controversy in the ancient world and, indeed, in later ages, but in this instance it contained an element of truth: by the second decade of the fifth century, Augustine had established himself as the leading theologian of the Latin-speaking world, to be ranked with the leading Greek Fathers. Had death not overtaken him, he would have been the outstanding Latin thinker at the Council of Ephesus in 431. He could not have been unaware that he was intellectually the superior of the Pelagians, and recognized as such in the Latin part of the Roman Empire, even if he was hardly known in the self-sufficient East—the Pelagian Controversy found no mention in the *Church History* of Socrates Scholasticus, which ended in 439.

There may well, however, have been a further factor determining Augustine's conduct in the Pelagian Controversy: personal alarm at what had been reported about the vindication of Pelagius's views at the Synod of Jerusalem of 415, which had been increased by the behavior of Pope

3. Aug., *serm.* 294,20,19. *PL* 39,1348.
4. Cyprian, *ep.* 64,5. *CSEL* 3(2),720–721.
5. Julian *apud* Aug., *op. imp.* 3,199. *CSEL* 85(1),498.

Zosimus in the period 417–18, when it appeared possible that Pelagius and Caelestius might be rehabilitated. Augustine's agitation is apparent in the sermon preached at Carthage on 23 September 417, in which he maintained that the Pelagian affair could not be reopened: *causa finita est.*

Argue with those [who speak against grace], and bring those who resist to us [bishops]. Two councils have sent their reports to the Apostolic See and replies have come from it. The case is concluded; would that the error might now end![6]

This language helps to explain Augustine's brutal rejection of Pelagius's overtures through Albina, Melania, and Pinianus in 418: he had been frightened, and was determined to impose his own understanding of the nature of grace and human redemption upon the Christian world. In the event he failed, the Massilian theologians of southern Gaul were not to be browbeaten into conformity with his views; but he has, down the ages, found many vociferous supporters.

The essence of Augustine's predestinarian theology was the conviction of the omnipotence of God, Who has created all things from nothing. This meant not only that all things depend for their existence on God, but that those who are endowed with minds—angels and men—are truly happy only when their wills are in harmony with God. Accordingly, if they seek to follow their own inclinations, and not God's will, they will be miserable. But more than that: God the Creator is a God of Justice, and if angels and men go against His will, they will rightly be punished. That was Adam's sin, and for that he deservedly died. It was here that the Pelagians stopped: Adam's death as a penalty affected only himself; his descendants die through a natural mortality. For Augustine, Adam's descendants were in his loins when he sinned, mysteriously participated in the sin, and so inherited the penalty. Moreover, because of this, they have lost all power to do good, unless enabled for every good

6. Aug., *serm.* 131,10: "Redarguite contradicentes, et resistentes ad nos perducite. Iam enim de hac causa duo concilia missa sunt ad sedem apostolicam: inde etiam rescripta venerunt. Causa finita est: utinam aliquando finiatur error." *PL* 38,734.

action by divine grace. But not all men receive grace, by God's most just decree and so, by an equally just decree, suffer an eternity of torment, without any regard to merit. Augustine accepts that this seems arbitrary and, to human reasoning, unjust, but holds that the reason for the divine decision will become clear on the Day of Judgment.

If left there, such a system would have no need for the work of Christ; but for Augustine, this would be impossible. For him, the Person and work of Christ were essential for healing the rupture between God and man brought about by the sin of Adam. *God was in Christ, reconciling the world to himself* (2 Cor. 5:19); but the reconciliation operates, since the Incarnation, in the sacrament of baptism, without which all human beings except the martyrs, who are a special case, are lost. For Augustine, no question of justice or injustice arises.

Significantly, Augustine's first anti-Pelagian treatise, *De Peccatorum Meritis et Remissione,* addressed to his friend, Count Marcellinus, was subtitled *De Baptismo Parvulorum;* and it was the implications of infant baptism—not the practice, which the Pelagians were quite ready to endorse, even though it was not yet a universal custom—that opened the controversy, together with Count Marcellinus's difficulty in understanding that, in this life, only Christ had lived without sin, that led Augustine to elaborate his doctrine of the grace of Christ. "God is One, and there is one mediator of God and men, the man Christ Jesus who has given Himself as the redemption for all men."[7] Augustine strengthened his case by quoting certain scriptural passages that supported his claims—and some were weighty—and by explaining away others, like 1 Timothy 2:4: *God willeth all men to be saved,* which seemed opposed to his thesis. The Pelagian position was less absolute. Julian of Eclanum, their ablest and wordiest apologist, appealed to the injustice of punishing individuals for an inherited sin which they were powerless to avoid. God cannot be anything but just. Quoting from Augustine's anti-Manichaean treatise *On the Two Souls,* Julian used Augustine's own definition of sin against its author:

7. *Sp. et litt.* 28,48: "Unus enim deus, unus est mediator Dei et hominum homo Christus Iesus, qui dedit seipsum redemptorem pro omnibus" (1 Tim. 2:5). *CSEL* 60,203.

"Sin is the will to do or to retain what justice forbids and from which we are free to abstain. . . . You say: 'Little ones are not weighed down by any sin of their own, but by the sin of another' . . . Your God is a persecutor of the newborn. With bad will He hands over to eternal fire little children who He knows could not have either a good or a bad will."[8] Julian's attitude is that of ordinary human morality, and later medieval opinion endorsed it in the conception of the *limbus infantium,* a place where the souls of unbaptized babies enjoy the highest natural happiness without beholding the beatific vision. Augustine's insistence on the necessity for baptism for membership of the Church with all its benefits had prevailed; but not to the total exclusion of charity to the helpless.

Distasteful as Augustine's views will seem to others than Julian of Eclanum, they are supported by quotations from Scripture, including the words of Christ Himself: *Many are called but few are chosen . . . The gate is narrow and the road is hard that leads to life, and there are few that find it.* Furthermore, it cannot be assumed that all Christians in the early Church were passionately concerned with the salvation of humanity as a whole. We have Julian the Apostate's testimony that, in his day, Christian liberality relieved pagan poverty and aroused great admiration for so doing;[9] but the fact that Christians discharged their religious duty in this life does not prove that they were necessarily filled with evangelistic enthusiasm for the conversion of their pagan neighbors as a whole. Pagan dislike for Christians was reciprocated. When in A.D. 203 Saints Perpetua and Felicity and their companions had their last meal on the night before their execution in the arena at Carthage, they threatened those who had come to watch them with God's judgment and ridiculed their curiosity.[10] When, in the fourth century, the Christians were in the ascendant, they had no hes-

8. Julian *apud* Aug., *op. imp.* 1,44; 48,2;4. *CSEL* 85 (1), 31;38; cf. 1,78; 1,82; 1,104; 2,38; 2,80; 2,187. *CSEL* 85 (1),93; 96; 121; 190; 219; 304.

9. *Misopogon* 363A. ed. Wright, Loeb Classical Library (London/Cambridge, Mass., 1959), II,488–90; *Letter* 22, 130 D. Wright (1961), III,70.

10. *Passio Sanctarum Perpetuae et Felicitatis,* 17: ". . . eadem constantia ad populum iactabant, comminantes iudicium Dei, contestantes passionis suae felicitatem, irridentes concurrentium curiositatem." In *The Acts of the Christian Martyrs,* ed. Herbert Musurillo (Oxford, 1972), 224.

itation in pulling down pagan temples. Artemius, the military commander in Egypt in 361, an aggressive Christian, made himself hated by the pagans of Alexandria by his spoliation of pagan shrines, for which he was duly executed by the Emperor Julian the Apostate in October 362. In his actions he had been enthusiastically supported by George of Cappadocia, the Arian bishop of Alexandria. In George's case the pagans did not wait for Julian to take action but, making alliance with the Catholics of Alexandria, who hated George as the enemy of St. Athanasius and a heretic, duly lynched him in December 361, for which they were mildly rebuked by Julian, whose primary concern was to get possession of George's extensive library rather than avenge its owner for having acted precipitately and outside the law. Martin of Tours made journeys around his diocese pulling down pagan temples. Certainly, the Church welcomed conversions, but accepted the belief in the damnation of those who died unbaptized without the faith and of sinful Christians who died within. On the other hand, Augustine's attitude to the fate of unbaptized infants was an extreme one, and not only to Julian of Eclanum. In the third century Tertullian had positively discouraged infant baptism: "Why hastens the age of innocence to the remission of sins?"[11] Tertullian was concerned with the awful implications of the baptismal promises and the risk to godparents *(sponsores)* if the children on whose behalf they had made the vows failed to carry them out. Augustine, being convinced that all human beings including infants have inherited the guilt of Adam's sin, insisted that, unless cleansed by baptism, they must infallibly be damned. This absolute need for baptism was a conclusion to which the minds of others of Augustine's contemporaries, like Gregory of Nyssa,[12] were moving.

Augustine's theology of the predicament of fallen humanity is deter-

11. Tertullian, *De Baptismo* 18,5: "Quid festinat innocens aetas ad remissionem peccatorum?" *CCL* 1,293; cf. Aug., *conf.* 1,11,18: "unde ergo etiam nunc de aliis et aliis sonat undique in auribus nostris: 'sine eum, faciat; nondum enim baptizatus est'?" *CSEL* 33,160. Tertullian would not have opposed infant baptism in an emergency, but did not share Augustine's view of the risk in deferring the sacrament. See *De Bapt.*, ed. Ernest Evans (London: SPCK, 1964), 101–2.

12. Gregory of Nyssa, *De eis qui baptismum differentibus*. *PG* 46,424C–425B.

mined by three principles. First, the omnipotence of God, Creator of all existing things from nothing. Secondly, the involvement of all humanity in Adam's sin and the guilt resulting from it. Finally, the helplessness of the sinner, as a result of the Fall, to do anything except evil without a direct and specific gift of grace, imparted by God without consideration of any individual merit. Some of this theology is derived particularly, it would appear, from Cyprian. What Augustine seems to have contributed, with portentous results, was the notion of an inherited legal liability, as opposed to moral weakness, by Adam's descendants, and a notion of a radical weakening of the human will which has left fallen man incapable of any good action without an immediate gift of divine grace. It is in this context that the notion of concupiscence becomes so important to Augustine, not simply in a sexual sense—though in that sense it certainly figures abundantly in his writings—but in a wider sense of a general moral weakness, which leaves the individual helpless to do anything of himself but evil.

The point here is, not that the individual is independent of God—since he is God's creation, all his powers derive from God—but how much the moral initiative with which Adam was endowed subsists in his descendants. The general feeling in the Greek East was that their ancestor's sin had left them weakened, but not powerless: they could sin, but could repent and try again. This was the view of Pelagius, and accounts for his reactions in 405 to a quotation from the *Confessions:* "Give what You command and command what You will!"[13]—words which Pelagius could not endure and barely restrained himself from entering into a furious argument with the bishop who had quoted them.[14] It was the view of Julian of Eclanum: "Free choice is as full after sin as it was before. I hold that human sin does not change the state of human nature, but the quality of human merit. There is in sinners the same nature of free choice to stop sinning as was present in them to allow them to turn away

13. Aug., *conf.* 10,29,40. *CSEL* 33,256.
14. Aug., *De dono Pers.* 20,53. *PL* 45,1026.

from righteousness."[15] Julian did not believe in Original Sin; his psychology was simplistic and he held that free will persisted in sinners, as Augustine himself had, in practice, to accept in his pastoral dealings, in the spirit of Dr. Johnson: "We *know* our will is free and *there's* an end on't."[16] Julian summed up his case very simply: "If these two truths are believed: that God's works are not evil nor His judgments unjust, the whole doctrine of Original Sin is crushed, just as if the impiety of inherited sin is accepted, these two: God's handiwork and His judgment, by which alone He can be known, are destroyed."[17] It is the reaction of the straightforward Christian believer. A similar reaction, though from the perspective of the asceticism of the Egyptian Desert, was that of the Massilian religious of southern Gaul. They agreed that God's grace could bring about a sudden change of heart in an individual; but they also held that an individual could himself make a decision.

The difference between such views and Augustine's ultimately turns on the consequences of Adam's sin on later human beings, and the consequences to the alienation of humanity from God, brought about by Adam's sin. This alienation was remedied by God Himself becoming fully man while remaining fully God and satisfying divine justice by His own human suffering. From then onward Augustine, the Pelagians, and the Semi-Pelagians of southern Gaul, were at one, or would have been if Augustine had not been so obdurate.

What was the reason for this hardness in a writer whom a Victorian admirer described as having a "rich, profound, and affectionate mind"? It has already been suggested that the attitude of Christians of Augustine's day towards pagans was often closer to that of pagans to Christians than to the spirit of the Gospel. To this should be added, in the case of Augustine, the conviction that, except in the case of the martyrs, there could be no possibility of salvation for those who had died unbaptized, which

15. Julian *apud* Aug., *op. imp.* 1,96. *CSEL* 85 (1).
16. Boswell, *Life of Dr. Johnson* 10 October 1769.
17. Julian *apud* Aug., *op. imp.* 4,2. *CSEL* 85(2),5.

immediately and inevitably consigned the vast majority of his fellow human beings to hell. A factor in Augustine's outlook, which has already been mentioned, is his emphasis on the acceptance of the texts of Scripture, which exclude Origen's universalism, which had already been condemned by the Church,[18] though in affirming the eternal suffering of the wicked, Augustine was prepared to allow the tender-hearted to suppose, "if the thought gives them pleasure, that the pains of the damned are, at certain intervals, in some degree, assuaged."[19] Too much should not, perhaps, be made of Augustine's interest in the question of how the material fires of hell could affect immaterial spirits,[20] which so disgusted J. B. Bury—this is the sort of discussion which would appeal to lettered men of the later Roman Empire, similar examples of which occur not infrequently in Augustine's writings. More disconcerting is his lack of interest in the suggestion that the saints in heaven may be moved to compassion at the sufferings of sinners in hell, an early example of a long-enduring belief in Christian circles that the deserved suffering of the wicked—the sight of thoroughly bad people getting their deserts—will arouse satisfaction in the minds of the elect.[21]

Augustine's seemingly callous indifference to this question is in marked contrast to his understanding of the significance of the Incarnation for humanity:

> Christ, who was the Only begotten Son of God by nature, was by mercy made the Son of Man for us, so that we, who are by nature sons of men, might be made sons of God by grace. For while remaining wholly unchanging in Himself, He received from us our nature, in which he could receive us, and while holding fast to His divinity, was made a sharer in our infirmity, so that we, being changed for the better, might lose what we are, being sinners and mortals, by participation in Him, who is immortal and righteous; and that we might preserve the good which He had done in our nature, made perfect by the supreme good in

18. Aug., *De Civitate Dei* 21,17. *CCL* 48,783; cf. 21,9. *CCL* 48,774–75.
19. *Enchiridion* 28,112. *CCL* 46,109.
20. *Civ.* 21,10,1. *CCL* 48,775–76.
21. John Rist, *Augustine: Ancient Thought Baptized* (Cambridge, 1994), 272.

the goodness of His nature. . . . Through the mediator between God and man, the man Christ Jesus, who was made partaker of our mortality to make us partakers of His divinity.[22]

And again:

We too were made by His grace what we were not, that is sons of God. Yet we were something else, and this much inferior, that is, sons of man. Therefore He descended that we might ascend, and remaining in His nature, was made a partaker of our nature, that we remaining in our nature might be made partakers of His nature. But not simply this; for His participation in our nature did not make Him worse, while participating in His nature makes us better.[23]

And yet again:

If He had not willed to be deformed, you would not have recovered the form which you lost. He, therefore, hung upon the cross, deformed; but this deformity was our beauty. In this life, therefore, let us hold the deformed Christ. What is the deformed Christ? *Far be it from me to glory, save in the cross of our Lord Jesus Christ, through which the world has been crucified unto me and I unto the world.* This is the deformity of Christ.[24]

These passages are some of many in which Augustine speaks of the deification of humanity, and they stand in a remarkable and rather dreadful contrast to his doctrine of the consequences of the Fall and the damnation of the overwhelming part of the human race. Another writer on deification, Gregory of Nyssa, has been accused of inheriting Origen's universalism. Why did Augustine not do likewise? There have been several answers to this question, including the effect of the "hot African sun,"[25] though some northern Europeans have found the sun of the east Mediterranean region at least as hot as that of North Africa! Perhaps the safest understanding of the opposition of these two theo-

22. Aug., *civ.* 21,15;16. *CCL* 48,781; 782.

23. Aug., *ep.* 140,4,10. *CSEL* 44,162.

24. Aug., *serm.* 27,6,6. *CCL* 41,365.

25. N. P. Williams, *The Ideas of the Fall and of Original Sin* (London, 1927), 330: "The crude lights and harsh shadows which the burning sun of Africa cast upon its desert sands seem to have sunk into the minds of Tertullian and Cyprian and to have been transmuted, as by some refracting medium, into the legalistic precision and the pitiless logic of Latin-Punic theology."

logical approaches is that Augustine's understanding of Adam's sin and its consequences was that of the African Church, as it had developed since St. Cyprian, with an added harshness which Augustine had himself taken from Scripture. Augustine's teaching on deification, on the other hand, whether it came from Eastern theology or was a development of a Latin theologian like Novatian, represents a potentially more optimistic view, though Augustine, no less than Novatian, was concerned with the Christian elect, and not with the generality of mankind. It is conceivable that if he had ever embarked upon a work like Gregory of Nyssa's *Catechetical Oration* he might have come to other, more hopeful conclusions about human destiny; but unlike the texts of Scripture which he was so very ready to cite, the African conception of the Two Cities seems to have dominated the mind of Augustine, so that there had to be a population for hell, made up of the fallen angels and the reprobate human beings. Under pressure, Augustine was to concede that unbaptized infants would suffer the mildest penalties in hell and that the degree of penal suffering by the damned would be proportionate to the quality of their offenses; but he refused to concede that hell would be anything but eternal.

This view inevitably affected his view of human freedom. In paradise Adam had been truly free, with a God-given freedom resembling that of the angels, which was capable of being abused, and in the event was abused, as the angelic freedom had been; but unlike the angels, humanity—or, more exactly, a small part of humanity—was elected to salvation by the inscrutable, but wholly just, decree of God. However, Adam's rebellion had so weakened human nature that man could only will evil, unless empowered to make every right decision by an immediate gift of God's grace.

In these circumstances, it is difficult to see how fallen man can be held responsible for his actions, as Augustine assumed. The Pelagians either denied any transmission of Original Sin or, like the Greek Fathers, saw it as weakening, rather than incapacitating, the human power of decision—a view which was shared by the ascetics of southern Gaul. Augustine left man helpless—*without me, ye can do nothing*—and so made clear the heroic character of God's plan of salvation: the Creator took upon Himself the nature of the created, as it had been before the Fall, suffered a human death and, by rising again, restored the unity between God and man broken by Adam. Yet—and this is the horrifying aspect of Augustine's theology—Christ's saving grace extended to only a tiny part of humanity. The overwhelming majority was excluded from its benefits by God's wholly just decree.

Perhaps one of the most extraordinary features of the history of Augustinianism is the way in which Augustine's predestinarian theology has been accepted by later theologians who were very far from lacking moral sensitivity. It would seem, indeed, that the mystery of God's decree has exercised an appeal over just and not uncharitable minds which were prepared to pass over the lack of charity in the mind of God Himself which is assumed. Christopher Dawson long ago spoke of the "intellectual conviction and the massive solidity of the Calvinistic theology," which is essentially Augustinian theology. It presents a system, a world outlook, which appeals to minds which desire one to explain the unhappy cosmos in which they find themselves—"I a stranger and afraid / In a world I never made." If it has features which appear to go against some texts of Scripture and ascribe to God an indifference to human ideas of justice and love, these can be met by an appeal to mystery: *For my plans are not your plans, nor are my ways your ways, declares the Lord; but as the heavens are high above the earth, so are my ways high above your ways, and my plans above your plans* (Is. 55:8–9). *How inscrutable are his judgments and his ways past finding out* (Rom. 11:33).

Yet despite its wide acceptance, Augustine's predeterminism is not his only influence; the literary career of the *Confessions* alone, the narrative of a soul seeking God, which has inspired so many generations of readers, from Ailred of Riveaux in the twelfth century to the Baron von Hügel in the twentieth, bears witness to Augustine's influence as a teacher of spirituality over the centuries. Predestinarianism did not, in the case of Augustine, lead him to religious passivity, but to the active pursuit of a God who had made humanity for Himself. It is this twofold aspect of Augustine: the dogmatic predestinarian and the seeker of God, the Doctor of Charity who continually insisted on the necessary damnation of the unbaptized—"no one is made a member of Christ, except either by baptism in Christ or by death for Christ"[26]—which constitutes the enigma of his personality. Not a little of the harshness which has shocked later generations may be ascribed to the Christianity of his age; but we may wonder that so large an intellect did not rise above it.

26. Aug., *De anima et eius origine* 1,9,10. *CSEL* 60,311.

CHAPTER I

THE PROBLEM

FEW STUDENTS OF Augustine's thought will be disposed to deny the harshness of the predestinarian teaching of the last twenty years of his life. From the composition of the *De Peccatorum Meritis et Remissione* in 411–12 to that of the *De Praedestinatione Sanctorum* in 429, Augustine's assertion of the helplessness of human nature to do anything good without the aid of divine grace is continually reaffirmed and intensified, and the books of the unfinished *Opus Imperfectum contra Iulianum* re-emphasize what had already been said two decades earlier, but with an added bitterness, inspired and sustained by Augustine's conviction that he was upholding the doctrine of the universal Church, and that those who did not subscribe to it not only maintained wrong belief but did so out of pride, the sin by which Satan fell. The reason for this conviction on Augustine's part is, no doubt, the interpretation which he found—or thought that he found—in many earlier Fathers, notably St. Cyprian and St. Ambrose; but it was sustained by personal emotion. Pelagius, in his *De Natura,* had buttressed his arguments by quotations from Augustine's earlier writings. Augustine was desperately concerned to maintain his own orthodoxy, by showing the agreement of his teaching with the tradition of the Church.

Augustine's brutality has shocked many readers and embarrassed not a few of his admirers, if only because it seems at variance with much of his other teaching, and especially with his understanding of the action of the Atonement. For Augustine, as for the Fathers in general, the purpose of the Incarnation was the salvation of fallen humanity. Christ is the Mediator, through whose humility we come to participate in His Divinity, not only by the remission of our sins but for the fulfillment of the destiny for which Adam was originally created. Christ raised human lowliness to the realms of the divine,[1] as well as suffering the penalty for fallen man; but the action of Christ in taking away the sin of the world is the work of the whole Trinity, and not only of the Son; for the works of the Trinity, although they may be ascribed to a particular Person, are not to be assigned to that one Person alone, for the three Persons of the Trinity are inseparable.[2] "As the Father and the Son and the Holy Spirit are inseparable, so they act inseparably. This is my faith, since it is the catholic faith."[3] Augustine's understanding of the Atonement is far removed from that parody of Christian belief put forward by some enemies, but also expressed by some Christians, that the Father, angered by human sin, is propitiated by the death of the Son who, being innocent, is a particularly pleasing sin-offering. Rather, Christ's death is a visible manifestation of the eternal self-offering of the Son to the Father in the bosom of the Trinity, in which the manhood of Christ participates through His assumption of human flesh,[4] so that humanity may become "the temple of God of the [human] gods (Ps. 81 [82]:6; John 10:34), whom He, the uncreated God, created."[5] The redemption of fallen man, then, does not simply restore him to the unfallen condition of Adam and Eve in para-

1. *Ep. Gal. exp.* 24,8: "Sic itaque unicus filius dei, mediator dei et hominum factus est, cum verbum dei deus apud deum et maiestatem suam usque ad humana deposuit et humilitatem humanam usque ad divina subvexit." *CSEL* 84,87.

2. *Enchiridion* 12,38: "An et quando unus trium in aliquo opere nominatur, universa operari trinitas intellegitur." *CCL* 46,71.

3. *De Trinitate* I,4,7: ". . . pater et filius et spiritus sanctus, sicut inseparabiles sunt, ita inseparabiliter operentur. Haec mea fides est, quando haec catholica fides." *CCL* 50,36.

4. *Ench.* 10,35: "quocirca in quantum deus est, ipse et pater unum sunt; in quantum autem homo est pater maior illo. . . . Ac per hoc et minor factus est et mansit aequalis, utrumque unus, sicut dictum est." *CCL* 46,49.

5. *Ench.* 15,56: "Unde nec tota nec ulla pars eius, vult [ecclesia] se coli pro deo, nec cuiquam esse deus pertinenti ad templum dei quod aedificatur ex diis quos facit non factus deus. . . . Deus ergo habitat in templo suo, non solum spiritus sanctus, sed etiam pater et filius; qui etiam de corpore suo per quod factus est caput ecclesiae, quae in hominibus est, ut sit ipse in omnibus primatum tenens, (Col. 1:18) ait: solvite *templum hoc, et in tribus diebus suscitabo illud* (Ioh. 2:19)." *CCL* 46,79; 80.

dise, though it does that as well;[6] it raises him to a peculiar dignity: "We have *fallen away in His anger;* but now, restored by Him and perfected by His greater grace, we shall be still and at leisure for eternity, seeing that He is God, and being filled by Him when He will be *all in all.*"[7]

This teaching appears to be very different from that of the later anti-Pelagian treatises; but its tragedy is that it is the destiny of only a very small proportion of the human race. "For since not all are being saved—indeed, by far the greater number are not—it may appear as if what God wishes to take place is not doing so because (as it seems) human will is impeding the will of God,"[8] since God wishes *all to be saved* (1 Tim. 2:4). This, of course, Augustine denies: those who seek to defy the decrees of God are actually performing His will, though they do not know it. However, it is clear to Augustine that far more are lost than are saved. "Although they are few in comparison with the lost, many are set free simply in number."[9] Augustine had no place for Origen's universalism, which taught the ultimate salvation of all creation.[10]

To most modern readers and to some in his own day,[11] Augustine's consignment of the overwhelming majority of the human race to perdition seems horrible; but what adds to the horror is the fact that, for most of the damned, there is no possibility of avoiding their fate, even if

6. *Ep. Gal. exp.* 30,6: "*Vt adoptionem,* inquit, *filiorum recipiamus. Adoptionem* propterea dicit ut distincte intelligamus unicum dei filium. Nos enim beneficio et dignitatione misericordiae eius filii dei sumus, ille natura est filius, qui hoc est quod pater." *CSEL* 50,96.

7. *Civ.* 22,30,4: "Quid enim sine illo fecimus, nisi quod *in ira eius* defecimus? (Ps. 89 [90]:9 LXX). A quo refecti et gratia maiore perfecti, vacabimus in aeternum, videntes quia ipse est Deus, quo pleni erimus quando *ipse erit omnia in omnibus* (1 Cor. 15:28)." *CCL* 48,865.

8. *Ench.* 24,97: "Cum enim non omnes, sed multo plures non fiunt salvi, videtur utique non fieri quod deus vult fieri, humana scilicet voluntate impediente voluntatem dei." *CCL* 46,100.

9. *Cor. et grat.* 10,28: "Quod ergo pauci in conparatione pereuntium, in suo vero numero multi liberantur, gratia fit, gratis fit, gratiae sunt agendae quia fit, ne quis velut de suis meritis, extollatur, se omne os obstruatur (Rom. 3:19), et qui gloriatur, in Domino glorietur." *PL* 44,933.

10. *Civ.* 21,17: ". . . Qua in re misericordior profecto fuit Origines, qui et ipsum diabolum atque angelos eius post gravora pro meritis et diuturniora supplicia ex illis cruciatibus eruendos et sociandos sanctis angelis credidit." *CCL* 48,783.

11. Julian of Eclanum is an obvious example.

they have heard the Gospel message and wish to be made Christian, unless they have received baptism. (There is an exception in the case of the martyrs, but only a few can belong to these.) Augustine's grounds for this teaching are based on the universal sinfulness of the human race. All sinned in Adam and rightly incurred the penalty. As a mark of His mercy, God allows the grace of baptism to a few; the rest of what Augustine calls "the lump of sin," the *massa damnata,* go to hell. Augustine defends his doctrine by appealing to the hidden justice of God: on the Last Day it will be made clear why one individual was taken and another left,[12] but this is hardly a reassurance to a troubled reader.

Nothing is gained by dwelling on this terrifying theology. What demands attention and some attempt at explanation is how Augustine came to formulate it, how he came to leave the individual apparently helpless in the hands of an angry God, whom he elsewhere sees as a God not simply of justice but of mercy and love, but who nevertheless apparently visits eternal penalties, not only for personal sins but for participation in the Fall by individuals who were, at the time, in the loins of Adam and had no consciousness of individuality, let alone any power of decision. Despite the long-continued, and very erudite, labors of Robert J. O'Connell to prove that Augustine had a theory of a pre-mundane fall of souls, few scholars have been persuaded,[13] and the traditional view for explaining human guilt in God's eyes as Adam's primal sin, in which, mysteriously, all have participated, continues to prevail. The flaws in this theology are clear, and we are faced with the problem of the intellectual grounds on which Augustine maintained and defended it. Clearly, he regarded the doctrine as that of the universal Church; but he wanted, as he always did, to find rational justification for a theology which he saw implied an apparently arbitrary decision on God's part to save one soul and to condemn another. In his own words: "The Apostle says: *What shall we say then? Is there injustice with God? God forbid!* For it does seem unfair that not

12. *Ench.* 24,95. *CCL* 46,99; cf. *grat. et lib. arb.* 23,45. *PL* 44,910.

13. For one who has, see Philip Cary, *Augustine's Invention of the Inner Self: The Legacy of a Christian Platonist* (Oxford University Press, 2000), xi–xii; but see also Gerald Bonner, *Journal of Theological Studies,* n.s. 52 (2001): 920–24.

on the basis of any merits of good and evil works God should love one and hate the other."[14] Augustine's immediate purpose was to prevent any possible reliance on good works as a cause for salvation and so commend humility to his readers; hence his frequent quotation of the Apostle: *O man, who art thou that repliest against God?* (Rom. 9:20), but this humility stems from man's nature: man is not self-existent but is created by God and utterly dependent upon God for his continued existence.[15] If God's sustaining power is ever taken away, humanity, like the world and all that therein is, will simply cease to be.[16]

"In the beginning God created the world out of nothing." This assertion has become so familiar to Christians over the centuries that it is difficult to appreciate its impact on the pagan world in which early Christianity grew up: a non-material God brings matter into existence from nothing. Such a conception was as difficult for Greco-Roman thought to accept as it is for many people today. In the classical world view, matter was eternally existent, as were the gods, and it was from eternally existent matter that the material world was shaped. This is the doctrine of Plato's *Timaeus.* Alternatively, it might be that the material world shaped itself. This was the view of Lucretius, who laid down the principle that "nothing can ever be created by divinity from nothing" *(nullam rem e nilo gigni divinitus umquam).* Lucretius's materialism did not prevail in the later centuries of the Roman Empire, but the notion of an eternally existent matter being shaped by the gods was still being proclaimed in the mid-fourth century A.D. in the handbook of pagan theology called by modern scholars *On the Gods and the World,* composed by Saturninus Salutius Secundus, friend of the emperor Julian the Apostate, by which time Christianity was on the margin of its victory over paganism, after which the doctrine of creation out of nothing triumphed in the now

14. *Ench.* 25,98: "*Quid enim dicimus?* ait [apostolus], *numquid iniquitas apud deum? Absit.* Iniquum enim videtur, ut sine ullis bonorum malorumve operum meritis unum deus diligit, oderit alterum." *CCL* 46,101.

15. See Pierre-Marie Hombert, *Gloria Gratiae: Se glorifier en Dieu, principe et fin de la théologie augustinienne de la grâce* (Paris: Institut d'Études Augustiniennes, 1996).

16. *Civ.* 12,[25]26: "quia nisi faciente [Deo], non tale vel tale esset, sed prorsus esse non posset." *CCL* 48,383.

dominant Christian Church in the Roman Empire.[17] In his sermon *De Fide et Symbolo (On Faith and the Creed),* preached to an African episcopal council at Hippo in 393, Augustine made a point of emphasizing (2,2–3) that God had created the world from nothing.

What were the consequences of the victory of creation from nothing for later Western theology? In the first place, it did away with the dualism which had formed the foundation of the Manichaean and other Gnostic systems. God had made everything in heaven and on earth, and there was no place for any opponent of equal power. This, of course, raised the problem of the existence of evil, which could now only be by the permissive will of God: *Does evil befall a city unless the Lord has done it?* (Amos 3:6). This was a question which concerned Augustine before he became a Manichee, and inspired a good deal of his thinking as a Catholic apologist, but the basic principle was clear: if God is the absolute ruler of the universe which He has created, and if what men call evil exists, then it can only be by His permissive will or, to borrow the words of Ronald Firbank: "The world is so dreadfully managed, one hardly knows to whom to complain."

Furthermore, the idea of creation from nothing affects the relationship between God and humanity. Because man is absolutely dependent upon God, there is no longer any place for the quasi-contractual relationship implied in the pagan dedicatory phrase *do ut des*—"I give in order that you may give." All that we have is from God and we can only offer Him what is already His own. Moreover God has logically and juridically absolute power over what He has made. Augustine was all too well convinced by St. Paul's adoption of Isaiah's question: *Does the clay say to him who fashions it: "What are you making?" or "Your work has no handles"?* (Is. 45:9; Rom. 9:20), and of the Pauline question to the individual who seeks comfort in his own good works: *What have you that you did not receive? If you received it, why do you boast as if it were not a gift?* (1 Cor. 4:7).

17. An English translation of Salutius is available in A. D. Nock, *Sallustius: Concerning the Gods and the Universe* (Cambridge, 1936).

Augustine's conception of the divine omnipotence comes out in his terrifying Letter 190, written in 418:

God by His creation has willed so many souls to be born who He foreknew would have no part in His grace, so that they might, by an incomparable multitude, outnumber those whom He has deigned to predestinate as children of promise in the glory of His kingdom, in order that it might be shown by the very multitude of the reprobate, that the number of those who are justly damned is of no concern with the righteous God. . . .[18]

Has the potter no right over the clay, to make out of the same lump one vessel for beauty and one for menial use? Shocking as Augustine's words are to many, they are essentially those of St. Paul.

What if God, desiring to show His wrath and to make known his power, has endured with much patience the vessels of wrath made for destruction, in order to make known the riches of his glory for the vessels of mercy, which he has prepared beforehand for mercy? (Rom. 9:22–23)

But, in contrast, there was a third consequence for Christian thinkers of the doctrine of creation from nothing: the introduction from pagan philosophical sources of the notion of divine providence *(pronoia, providentia),* found in some pagan philosophical sources but claimed and emphasized by Christian thinkers. God is not an irrational artist who creates and governs by impulse. He is a reasonable being, Reason itself, who creates and continues to govern His creation in every detail, from the smallest part to the greatest. Augustine's encomium on God's providence in Book V of *The City of God* is too long to be cited in its entirety, but its conclusion sums up the whole:

[God] has left neither heaven nor earth, nor angel nor man, nor the organs of the least and puniest living creature, nor the flower's bud nor the tree's leaf, without the harmonious arrangement of these several parts and a certain easeful peace. It cannot possibly be believed that He could have willed to leave the kingdoms of men without laws of His own providing for their guidance and government.[19]

18. *Ep.* 190,3,12. *CSEL* 57,146–47.
19. *Civ.* 5,11. *CCL* 47,142. Tr. Wand.

This is reassuring for the Christian believer who trusts in God; but it also proclaims a restriction on the human will to effect anything contrary to the divine intention. In the last book of *The City of God,* Augustine expresses his conviction clearly:

> Evil men do many things contrary to the will of God, but so great is His wisdom and so great His power that all things which seem to oppose His will tend towards those results which He Himself has foreknown as good and just.[20]

Finally, we may regard as a possible product of belief in creation from nothing Augustine's emphasis on the wrath of God upon the children of disobedience. In certain religious systems there are accounts of how human beings incur the wrath of a god or the gods and are punished, justly or unjustly, for their offenses; but the notion of the whole human race being deservedly under the just judgment of God is particularly Christian, stemming from the conviction of the heinous nature of the primal sin by Adam, which might so easily have been avoided, and thus constituted an act of rebellion altogether out of proportion to the actual gravity of the offense committed. Augustine unhesitatingly adopted this conviction in its extreme form and assumed the damnation of unbaptized children as a rightful judgment on their participation in Adam's sin, while admitting the mystery of the divine decision.

> Two little children are born. If you ask what is due, they both cleave to *the lump of perdition*. But why does its mother carry the one to grace, while the other is suffocated by its mother in her sleep? Both have deserved nothing of good, but the *potter has power over the clay, of the same lump to make one vessel unto honor and another to dishonor. . . . Oh the depth of the riches of the wisdom and knowledge of God! How unsearchable are His judgments and His ways past finding out!*[21]

Such language, which is constantly repeated in Augustine's later writings, has persuaded many students that he ended his life as a complete supralapsarian predestinarian theologian, a hypercalvinist before Calvin was born: God, it is asserted, created certain men and women for damnation to His own greater glory. In fact Augustine's thinking, although it

20. *Civ.* 22,2. *CCL* 48,807. Tr. Bettenson; cf. *Ench.* 46,100. *CCL* 46,103.
21. *Serm.* 26,13. *CCL* 41,357.

made no difference to the fate of the damned, was more subtle. God created all things from nothing. Within creation were two classes of beings that differ from all others because they had the enlightenment of reason, and could therefore choose whether to serve God or their own desires: angels and human beings. For angels, the choice to obey God was made before the creation of the world, and they are now saved or damned everlastingly. Accordingly, they differ from humanity in that the good angels do not need a mediator, since they cannot now fall,[22] while the fallen angels do not get one.[23] For the human race, existing in the loins of Adam, the case was otherwise. Adam was created with free choice. Humanity sinned in him, was justly condemned to eternal punishment, and, in this life, lost its original endowment of free choice. Fallen man, lacking divine grace, can only choose to do evil. He is a slave to sin.

This is Augustine's mature judgment. However, there is ample material in earlier parts of his voluminous writings which implies that man possesses free will and it is possible to speak of Augustine as a "philosopher of freedom,"[24] in contrast to the Manichaean view that the evil element in man constrains him to evildoing, from which constraint he can be freed only by seeking liberation from the flesh by rigorous asceticism. What, however, must be borne in mind is that, in proclaiming human liberty against the Manichees, Augustine was concerned with Adam's condition before the Fall. Augustine's final break with Pelagius came about when he read Pelagius's work *On Nature* and there found that Pelagius was using Augustine's anti-Manichaean arguments referring to human nature before the Fall to support his own contention that there had been no Fall. Either by accident or design, Pelagius ignored Augustine's fundamental distinction between free will before and after the Fall. I am inclined to think that it was by accident. I can offer no evidence, apart from the fortuitous character of the availability of books in

22. *Ep. Gal. exp.* 24,5–6: "Angeli porro, qui non lapsi sunt a conspectu dei, mediatore non opus habent, per quem reconcilientur. (6) Item angeli, qui nullo suadenti spontanea praevaricatione sic lapsi sunt, per mediatorem non reconcililantur." *CSEL* 84,80.

23. *Ench.* 15,57. *CCL* 46,80.

24. Mary Clark, *Augustine: Philosopher of Freedom* (New York, 1958).

the Roman world and a reluctance to assume that Pelagius would have deliberately suppressed a decisive change in Augustine's thinking, if he had known it. He might quibble and prevaricate in his own interest, as he seems to have done at the Councils of Jerusalem and Diospolis in 415, but this is not the same as deliberately suppressing evidence in a theological treatise.

There is no doubt about Augustine's final position on predestination in the field of dogmatic theology; but there is another, and very influential, field of his teaching where the position is less clear: that of his spirituality, where the notion of the soul seeking God by an exercise of the intellect and rising to the heights of contemplation is clearly expressed. This is particularly marked in the *Confessions,* which is the account of a human soul searching for God, as revealed in the case of a particular individual. When Augustine came to write the *Confessions,* he had come to accept the absolute primacy of divine grace in motivating all our thoughts and intentions, as well as providing the power to act, and had in this way passed beyond the Neoplatonism which had so excited him at Milan in 396. It seems equally clear that in the *Confessions* Augustine is writing both as a theologian and as a philosopher, simultaneously "proving the existence of God [and] developing a theory of cognition,"[25] but there can be no doubt about the significance of that most quoted of all Augustine's sayings: "Thou hast made us for Thyself and our heart has no rest until it may repose in Thee." The human soul is drawn to God and yearns for God—in his *Commentary on the First Epistle of St. John* Augustine declares that "all the life of a good Christian is a holy desire. What you desire, you do not yet see; but desiring makes you able to be filled *(capax),* so that when that which you are to see comes, you may be filled."[26] Despite the Fall, the attraction of God remains in the human soul. The tragedy is that so many souls are distracted from the true

25. Étienne Gilson, *Introduction à l'étude de saint Augustin* (Paris, 1969), 311–12.

26. *Ep. Ioh. tr.* 4,6: "Tota vita christiani boni, sanctum desiderium est. Quod autem desideras, nondum videas; sed desiderando capax effeceris ut cum veneris quod videas, implearis." *PL* 35,2008–9.

source of their happiness by the transitory and deluding pleasures of this world.

The fact that there is a natural yearning for God in the human soul does not, however, establish that the fallen soul can do anything to satisfy that yearning without a specific impulse from the grace of God. This was what lay at the heart of Augustine's contention with Pelagianism. Pelagius held that there were in a good action three elements: the power to do it; the will to do it; and the performance of the action itself. God, he said, had given us the power; the will and the performance come from us.[27] This Augustine denied to be the case with fallen humanity. The power and the will to do good are both enfeebled and each required a specific impulsion to be effective. Lacking this impulsion we are helpless to do anything good, although we are left free to do evil, a freedom which is in fact slavery, because we are slaves to sin.

It is here that we may briefly notice the theory put forward by the Swedish theologian Anders Nygren in his powerful, if controversial, study called in English *Agape and Eros,* of which the English translation appeared in the years 1932–39. Nygren was a learned and imaginative thinker, but an exceedingly arbitrary one—a critic, John Burnaby, observed that the book "suffers from its unnecessary and quite unjustified claim to historical objectivity."[28] To attempt to present in a few words a theme of a work which in translation comes to 741 pages of text is obviously presumptuous, but for our purposes, in noticing Nygren's treatment of Augustine, it must be attempted. Nygren's case rests on making a radical distinction between Agape, the spontaneous and unmotivated love of the Gospels, God's gift, and the only initiator of fellowship with God,[29] for *"there is from man's side no way at all that leads to God,"*[30] while

27. *Grat. Christ. et pecc.orig.* I,4,5. *CSEL* 42,127–8.

28. John Burnaby, *Amor Dei: A Study of the Religion of St. Augustine* (London, 1938), 15.

29. Nygren, *Agape and Eros,* trans. Philip S. Watson (London: SPCK, 1982), 80: "There is . . . no way for man to come to God, but only a way for God to come to man: the way of Divine forgiveness, Divine love."

30. Ibid. Italics Nygren's.

Eros, on the other hand, is love for the Beautiful and the Good, discussed by Plato in the *Phaedrus* and the *Symposium*. "Eros is the 'love of desire', or acquisitive love; Eros is man's way to the Divine; Eros is egocentric love."[31] "Of such a love," says Nygren, "it could scarcely be said that it 'seeketh not its own.'"[32]

Clearly, by Nygren's definition, Agape and Eros are incompatible; yet he asserted that Augustine combined them in his concept of *caritas*. "The meeting of the Eros and Agape motifs in Augustine's doctrine of *Caritas* is thus not merely one point among others: it concerns the very heart of his conception of Christianity."[33] According to Nygren: "Neoplatonism never ceased to be an important factor in [Augustine's] spiritual life, even after he became a Christian."[34] "The *Confessions* . . . reveal the immediate significance of Eros and Agape for [Augustine's] religious life."[35] His conversion "produced no essential change. It falls entirely within the framework created by Eros piety."[36] "The descent of God in Christ to lost humanity is of the utmost importance; and yet it has *no intrinsic value* for Augustine. In other words, *Augustine is not really interested in the causal, but only in the teleological, motivation of the Incarnation,*" not, that is, with the unbounded love of God but with the mechanism determined for man's salvation.[37]

Nygren's contentions were criticized by John Burnaby in his study *Amor Dei*. Burnaby declined to accept Nygren's radical opposition of Platonism and Christianity. "[Augustine's] Platonism," he wrote, "is Christian because he finds the Supreme Value and the most compelling loveliness in the love which is God's own being; and because he believes that *amor Dei* is God's gift of Himself to His children,"[38] and he pointed to

31. Ibid., p. 175.
32. Ibid., p. 181.
33. Ibid., p. 457.
34. Ibid., p. 462.
35. Ibid., p. 463.
36. Ibid., p. 465.
37. Ibid., p. 529: "The descent of God in Christ to lost humanity is of the utmost importance; and yet it has *no intrinsic value* for Augustine. In other words, *Augustine is not really interested in the causal, but only in the teleological motivation of the Incarnation*. . . . The teleological consideration also maintains, it is true, that the Incarnation is the revelation of Divine love, but the main point is that this has happened in order that we may be enabled to ascend to [God]." Italics Nygren's.
38. Burnaby, *Amor Dei*, p. vi.

a radical deficiency in Nygren's whole argument: "Eros and Agape are not the only Greek words for love. The *Philia* in which Aristotle discovered the richest endowment of the human personality is a stranger neither to the Old Testament nor to the New . . . and Nygren, with a candour which we may admire, owns that he can make nothing of it."[39] In this context, a single section of Augustine's *Enchiridion*[40] makes nonsense of Nygren's interpretation; for here Augustine uses all three Latin words for love: *caritas, amor,* and *dilectio,* apparently interchangeably, and not in the special sense which Nygren ascribes to *caritas.* It is important to know when an ancient author uses a word in a technical sense; but it should not too readily be assumed that he uses it with the precision of a modern writer, rather than as an alternative to another word with a similar meaning for stylistic reasons. Augustine was, after all, a rhetorician, not a modern technical philosopher.

The important fact, however, is not Nygren's dogmatic and prejudiced interpretation of Augustine, but his attempt to find in Augustine a will to ascribe to the human soul, even in its fallen condition, an aspiration to God, a movement to seek Him. The crucial question here, as we shall see, concerns the origin of this movement: does it come directly and entirely from God, or does the fallen human soul retain some initiative? This was the issue in Augustine's debate with the Semi-Pelagians, and his final view is clear: the initiative lies entirely with God. Augustine had not, however, always held that view; and in his spiritual writings there is recognition of an instinct in the human soul to seek God, which led Abbot Butler of Downside Abbey to call Augustine, in a wholly favorable sense, the "Prince of Mystics."[41] These two paradoxical aspects of Augustine's thought will be the theme of our following chapters. It

39. Burnaby, *Amor Dei,* 18; cf. Nygren, *Agape and Eros,* p. 92: "Nor is there any room for the 'love of friendship' in a theocentric relationship to God, for that love presupposes an equality between Divine and human love which does not exist. It is excluded by the sovereignty of Divine love."

40. *Ench.* 31,117. *CCL* 46,111–22. Nygren, curiously, was aware of this, *Agape and Eros,* p. 557: "The three terms, *amor, dilectio* and *caritas,* are used quite indifferently."

41. Cuthbert Butler, *Western Mysticism: The Teaching of Augustine, Gregory and Bernard on Contemplation and the Contemplative Life,* 3rd ed. (London, 1967), 20.

remains for us here to attempt to clarify the contribution of Platonism and Christianity to Augustine's spiritual thinking.

The influence of Platonism upon Augustine is unquestionable, whether one approves of it or not. The fact that Augustine's teachers were Plotinus and Porphyry rather than Plato himself, and that he read them in Latin translation rather than in the original Greek, should not deter us from numbering him among Plato's disciples. Some theologians, Nygren among them, have seen Augustine's Platonism as being at variance with his Christianity; more have considered much of the teaching of Plato to be in harmony with the Gospels. Augustine himself never disowned the inspiration which he received from reading the Platonists at Milan in 385–86 in helping to destroy the remnants of Manichaeism in his thinking and bringing him to the acceptance of catholic Christianity. In the *De Doctrina Christiana* (II,40,60) he commended the study of the Platonists to Christian readers, when they declare truths in harmony with the Christian faith. Augustine, like many other Christian theologians, did not limit truth exclusively to revelation. *The wind blows where it wills.*

There are two notions which govern Augustine's understanding of the spiritual progress of the soul. The first is participation. This is a Platonic conception *(metousia, metoche),* which derives from the belief that existent beings owe their existence from participation in the eternal Forms. This notion Augustine took over, conceiving of the Forms as thoughts in the mind of God.[42] The human soul is not made blessed, and cannot be good or happy by its own efforts, but only by participation in God. (This is the foundation of Augustine's doctrine of deification, which will be discussed later.) If the soul turns away from God by pride, as it did in the Fall,[43] then it becomes, as it were, chilled and numb; if it returns to Him,

42. *De diversis Quaestionibus octoginta-tribus,* q. 46,2: "Sunt namque ideae principales quaedam formae vel rationes rerum stabiles atque incommutabiles, quae ipsae formatae non sunt, ac per hoc aeternae ac semper eodem modo sese habentes, quae divina intellegentia continentur. Et cum ipsae neque oriantur neque intereant, secundum eas tamen formari dicitur omne quod oriri et interire potest et omne quod oritur et interit." *CCL* 44A,71.

43. *Ep.* 140,31,74; "Animae igitur rationalis mutabilitas admonetur, quo noverit, nisi

it is illuminated by the divine light and warmed by a spiritual heat.[44] So Augustine declares in a sermon:

> As human beings render to Caesar what belongs to Caesar, when they hand back to Caesar the coin which bears his image, so do they render to God what belongs to God when they give themselves back to Him whose image they bear and lift their minds above to their designer, to the light from which they came and to the spiritual fire which warms them. If they withdraw from it they grow cold, if they move away they sink into darkness. But if they return to that light, that fire, they are illuminated.[45]

Accordingly, the progress of the soul should be towards a closer and closer participation in God, which will be completed only in the next life, when it will be as close a union with God as is possible for a created being with its Creator.

The other concept, which goes with participation, is the Pauline doctrine of the restoration of the image of God in the human soul, which has been defiled and darkened by the withdrawal from God effected by the Fall. Augustine's starting point is Genesis 1:26: *Let us make man in our own image and likeness.* In his *Uncompleted Commentary on Genesis,* begun about 393 and only partially completed in 426 or 427, Augustine finds three principles established by this text: (1) that the creation of Adam was the work of the whole Trinity (16,55); (2) that an image is not merely like its model: if it is to be an image it must be "born" of its model—there must be a direct relationship between them (16,57); and, finally (3), that "likeness" *(similitudo)* is consequent upon participation (16,58). An individual becomes "like" God by participating in Him, and he is able to do this because he is a "spiritual being" *(rationalis substantia),* made by God without any intervening nature (16,60). When he came to com-

participatione incommutabilis boni iustam, salvam, sapientem, beatam se esse non posse, nec sibi eam bonum esse posse propria voluntate sed malum. Propria quippe voluntate avertitur a bono incommutabili eaque aversione vitiatur; nec sanari per se ipsam potest sed gratuita misericordia sui creatoris, quae in hac vita eam ex fide viventem in spe constituit salutis aeternae." *CSEL* 44,221.

44. Ibid., 22,55; 23,56–57. *CSEL* 44,201; 202–204.

45. *En. Ps. 103, serm.* 4,2. Tr. Maria Boulding. *CCL* 40,1522.

plete the *Uncompleted Commentary* at the end of his life, Augustine was to explain that God the Son was the only true image of the Father, because He was coeternal and of the same nature. Man, being a created being, could only be a partial image of God, even if he had not sinned (16,61), but he was in God's likeness. Even though, through the Fall, he had fallen away into what Augustine calls "the region of unlikeness" *(regio dissimilitudinis)*[46]—a phrase inspired by Platonic thought[47]—he can be restored after baptism to the full image of likeness by participation in God. This is brought about by membership of the Church, which is the Body of Christ, and which Christ, the true High Priest and minister of the sacrament, offers to the Father in the Eucharist. Augustine, in a sermon preached to the newly baptized on the morning of Easter Sunday, expresses his notion of how each individual communicant is offered to God.

> The bread which you can see on the altar, sanctified by the word of God, is the body of Christ. The cup, or rather what the cup contains, sanctified by the word of God, is the blood of Christ. It was by means of these things the Lord Christ wished to present us with His body and blood, which He shed for our sake for the forgiveness of sins. If you receive them well, you are yourselves what you receive. You see, the Apostle says: *We, being many, are one loaf, one body* (1 Cor. 10:17). That's how he explained the sacrament of the Lord's table; one loaf, one body, is what we all are, many though we be.[48]

The Eucharist is a mystery. The grains of wheat and the individual grapes represent individual Christians. They are ground and pressed to make the bread and the wine. By consecration they become the Body and Blood of Christ, by partaking of which the believer is made part of the one Body, the Church; and it is by Christ, through membership of the Church, that the faithful Christian comes, at last, to the eternal blessedness of the Vision of God.

46. *Conf.* 7,10,16. *CSEL* 33,157.

47. See P. Courcelle, *Les Confessions de saint Augustin dans la tradition littéraire* (Paris, 1963), appendix 5: "Répertoire des textes relatifs à la 'région de dissemblance' de Platon à Gide," pp. 623–40.

48. *Serm.* 227. *PL* 38,1246–47. Tr. Hill, 3/6,254.

But this comes about by the grace of God and not by any works of the believer. "All the life of a good Christian is nothing else but holy desire";[49] but can the desire of the individual who yearns to come to God play any part in initiating this progress? There is a paradox between Augustine's predestinarian teaching and the aspiration of the human soul to God which led Abbot Butler to call Augustine the Prince of Mystics. These two paradoxical aspects of Augustine's thought will be the theme of the following chapters.

49. *Ep. Io. ad Parthos tr.* I,4,6. *PL* 35,2008.

CHAPTER 2

THE EVIDENCE

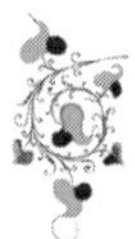

AUGUSTINE OF HIPPO may be regarded as a major writer, not only in a qualitative, but in a quantitative sense. To look upon his collected works with a view to reading them is an awe-inspiring experience; to realize that he not merely read, but actually wrote them, is overwhelming, the more so when we remember how much of his time was devoted to his diocese which, in contemporary terms, was more like a large and busy modern parish. He had, it is true, his household clergy, to whom he delegated all financial business.[1] How much they were available to help his literary labors by checking references and proofreading we do not know, but his demands must have been formidable, since he not infrequently had several literary pieces in hand at one and the same time. It would be fascinating if one could see what Augustine's study at Hippo was like. Did he have, as a certain English scholar of an earlier generation is reputed to have had,[2] a number of tables, each one devoted to a different book? Were there notebooks and scraps of parchment bearing references? Presumably, judging from his language, he must have had to turn from one composition to another,[3] while keeping in mind the thread of each successive argument; but even more demanding and remarkable was the labor involved in compiling the two books of the *Retractations* in 427, when Augustine passed in review almost all his larger

1. Possidius, *Vita Augustini*, 24. Michele Pellegrino, ed., *Vita di S. Agostino* (Edizioni Paolini, 1955), 124–32.

2. K. Lowther Clark.

3. See *ep.* 169,4,13. *CSEL* 44,620–22.

compositions to that date, indicating where he had changed his mind and defending himself against criticism where he had not.[4] John Burnaby, in a well-known paper delivered at the Augustinian Congress at Paris in 1954, calculated that there was a larger amount of defense than of withdrawal in the *Retractations* than is commonly assumed;[5] but the great interest for us is Augustine's power of memory in reconsidering his compositions. Did he re-read them all?—a lengthy business. Had he kept notes of questions and criticisms over the years? We do not know; but the composition of the *Retractations* was unquestionably a major undertaking, and has been of immense value to later students of Augustine's writings.

The range, and not only the quantity, of Augustine's literary output was immense and covered very different topics and opponents. Furthermore, the *method* of composition—dictation, as was the custom of the times, often to answer a particular problem raised by a particular individual, or to treat of a particular text of Scripture—could mean that there were occasional inconsistencies in his compositions. Perhaps one of the most impressive things about Augustine's writings as a whole is the way in which various parts hold together, often with a remarkable consistency. There was, indeed, one major change in his outlook on human freedom, which will be the theme of the present chapter. In the meantime, let us consider two features of Augustine's general approach to theological thinking and theological disputation which are characteristic at all times.

The first is his general view of the cosmos under the divine rule, a belief in its order and harmony, even when the facts appear otherwise. One might call it an aesthetic approach, and it is worth remembering that his first literary publication, composed when he was still a Manichee, was

4. See the study by J. de Ghellinck, *Patristique et Moyen Age: Études histoire littéraire et doctrinale.* Tom. III: *Compléments à l'étude de la Patristique* (Brussels/Paris, 1948), Étude VIII: "Une édition patristique célèbre," 339–65.

5. Burnaby, "The *'Retractations'* of St. Augustine: Self-criticism or Apologia?" *Augustinus Magister,* Congrès internationale augustinien (Paris, 21–24 September 1954), vol. 1, 85–92.

De Pulchro et Apto (On the Beautiful and the Fitting), in which "beauty" was regarded as a quality in an object inherent in itself, "fitness" as a quality in its relation to other objects. The *De Pulchro et Apto* is sometimes seen as expressing Manichaean philosophy, but it expresses an outlook which was to affect Augustine's thinking all his life. As a Manichee he could regard many elements in the material world as the work of the Prince of Darkness, and therefore ugly in themselves and in their relation to the good. As a catholic Christian, believing that God was the sole creator, and that all that God had created was *very good* (Gn. 1:31), he could no longer hold that view. However, he argued that what may appear to be ugly in itself, and therefore evil, might be beautiful in its relation to other things. In his early treatise *On Order* he used as an example the case of a mosaic, a particularly favored artistic creation in the late Roman world. The individual cubes *(tessellae)* are differently colored. A critic who looked at one particular cube and did not like it, ignoring its place in the pattern as a whole, and then blamed the artist as lacking in judgment, resembles the ignorant person who fails to see order and harmony in the universe as a whole because of one feature which displeases him.[6] Augustine carried this mode of thinking very far, when discussing the ordering of human society. Thus, in *De Ordine* he affirms the need for the public executioner who, though himself horrible, cruel, and evil, ensures order in a city by afflicting evildoers, and goes on, even more startlingly, to defend the social rôle of the prostitute: "Expel the harlot from society and lust will reign everywhere. Put her in the place of married women, you will soil everything with shame and dishonor. Thus these women live a most vile life by their profession; but they have their place by the laws of order, even though it is a very vile one."[7] Augustine came in his later career to deplore the use of capital punishment and to condemn prostitution; but his recognition of the need for a well-ordered

6. *Ord.* 1,1,2. *CCL* 29,90; cf. *civ.* 11,23. *CCL* 48,341–43. See A.-I. Bouton-Touloubic, *L'ordre caché: La notion d'ordre chez saint Augustin* (Paris, 2002).

7. *Ord.* 2,4,12. *CCL* 29,114.

society in the life of the present world continued to have eloquent expression in Book XIX of *The City of God:*

> Similarly the Earthly City, which does not live by faith, seeks an earthly peace, and pins down to a particular purpose the agreement of its citizens, whether they command or obey, the purpose being that the wills of men may achieve a measure of concordance as regards the things which pertain to this mortal life.[8]

In the supernatural order, however, there is no need of any compromise, and Augustine can declare, with terrifying complacency:

> Even the eternal fire which is to torment the ungodly is not an evil thing. It has its own measure, form, and order, debased by no iniquity. But torment is evil for the damned, for whose sins it is the due reward. Nor is light an evil thing because it hurts the weak-eyed.[9]

These words, written in 405, were echoed in Book XII of *The City of God,* to be dated to 418.[10] They show how much of what I have called aesthetic considerations underlies Augustine's notions of the government of the cosmos. Hellfire has its own measure, form, and order *(modus, species, ordo)*—words which Augustine frequently uses to define the operation and the work of reason, which make the world beautiful; but hellfire also plays its moral part in fulfilling God's decree by tormenting sinners. Augustine never questioned the biblical notion of eternal punishment, any more than did most of his contemporaries, and devotes space in *The City of God*[11] to an attempt to explain why it should be morally acceptable for God to inflict eternal punishment for sins committed in time. What however is to be emphasized is how this notion of God as the supreme artist would have strengthened Augustine's image of God the Creator from nothing. God had created everything good, but the creation as a whole was *very good:* the whole is greater than the sum of the parts. Accordingly, it was easier to accept apparent blemish-

8. *Civ.* 19,17. *CCL* 48,684. Tr. Barrow.
9. *Nat. bon.* 38. *CSEL* 25/2,873.
10. *Civ.* 12,4. *CCL* 48,358–9.
11. *Civ.* 21,11. *CCL* 48,775–6.

es in creation, from the fall of the sparrow to the loss of a human soul, as part of the divine plan and contributing to its beauty.

Secondly—though to what extent it helps to illuminate Augustine's intellectual development can only be a matter of individual judgment—there is the unhappy fact that in all his major controversies Augustine began by friendly overtures but ended with bitter words: with the Manichees, whose Elect he eventually accused of indulging in private in obscene rites, while admitting that as a Manichaean Auditor he had not witnessed any impropriety; with the Donatists, when he defended coercion by the secular state in singularly harsh language; and with the Pelagians. While recognizing that his various disputes lasted over periods of years, so that Augustine's restraint was only gradually eroded, though he never descended to the sort of abuse which St. Athanasius levelled against the dead emperor Constantius, and which seems to have come almost naturally to Jerome, Augustine's eventual loss of charity toward successive opponents must be deplored. Here again, however, the notion that the suppression of heresy was a duty owed by the faithful to God would have harmonized with his belief in the action of divine providence in the administration of human affairs, and with an increasing tendency to regard as heresy any departure from the norm of what Augustine regarded as right belief. It would be useful to know more about the effect on Augustine of the anti-Origenistic crusade launched in the East by Theophilus of Alexandria, which culminated in the condemnation of Origen's teaching by Pope Anastasius in 400. Despite the campaign against him, many people continued to recognize and to respect Origen's theological greatness. Augustine himself wrote against Origen's teaching, particularly that on creation and universal salvation; but he refers to him in *The City of God* with respect as a man *doctus et exercitatus*—"learned and experienced"[12]—without any of the violent hostility which Jerome entertained for him after 390.

Augustine's familiarity with Origen was far less than Jerome's, to

12. Ibid. 11,23: "hominem . . . tam doctum et exercitatum." *CCL* 48,342.

whom indeed he owed much of his knowledge; but his thinking increasingly diverged from what he knew of Origen's thought, with its emphasis on human freedom. In his earlier writings against the Manichees, Augustine had urged the natural freedom of human nature at the creation of Adam, as against the Manichaean belief that human beings are an amalgam of light and darkness, good and evil, and the evil, material side of human nature causes us to sin. Against this Augustine maintained that in Eden Adam was created wholly good and fell into sin by the wrong exercise of his free will, a midway force *(media vis)*[13] which was entirely within his control, to be used or abused as he should determine. Adam chose to misuse it and fell; but what did the Fall imply? Whatever its effect, it did not cause Adam and Eve to pass out of existence. They became liable to the death of the body and, more terribly, after physical death to the eternally living death of the soul in hell. But, in this world, some vestige of man's paradisal nature remained. Weakened and infirm, with the image of God in the soul darkened and distorted, humanity, through its participation in God, still retains traces of its heavenly origins, and the freedom to choose was maintained by Augustine against the Manichaean assertion of the inevitability of sin.

It is to be admitted that theologians, like other people, are often inconsistent in applying their principles to everyday life. The Manichees affirmed human helplessness to avoid sinning because of an evil element within, but the Elect, by a stern code of moral conduct and by the consumption of foods containing particles of heavenly light, were believed in time to attain to a state of sanctity. Equally, in pastoral practice most Christian predestinarians act as if the individual has free will. That free will is, however, a gift of God in the individual's creation. Since we are not self-existent we are, in the last resort, wholly dependent, unless God should concede to us an element of independence. But a further problem arises. If we believe that God is omniscient, that He knows all that

13. *Sp. et litt.* 33,58.: "... liberum arbitrium naturaliter adtributum a creatore animae rationali, illa media vis est, quae vel intendi ad fidem, vel inclinari ad infidelitatem potest." *CSEL* 60,216.

has been, is, and will be, does His foreknowledge constrain us to act as He foresees? This was to be a major concern of Augustine, to be discussed at length in the eleventh book of the *Confessions,* in which Augustine maintained that God is outside time, which is His own creation, so that for Him past, present, and future exist as an eternal present.[14] Augustine's notion that for God time is an eternal present has been criticized by at least one scholar[15] as being not properly Christian—the Bible speaks of God as One who is, and was, and is to come (Rev. 1:13). Augustine's theory is drawn from Plotinus (*Enneads* 3,7,3), Whether or not Augustine was justified in adopting a non-biblical concept to explain Christian doctrine must be a matter of opinion. Augustine might reply from his side that to speak of God in terms of present, past, and future, as the text of Revelation does, is to describe Him in His relations with the world and not in the consciousness of His eternal being.

At all events, granted the premise of God's foreknowledge, as most Christians do, the question of human choice inevitably arises: can choice be free, in any real sense, if God already knows what we are going to do in our future? The notion of God seeing the created world as an eternal present seems to allow some element of free choice: if God sees us acting, He does not constrain us to act. However, for us the future is yet to be—it might be said that it is, as yet, non-existent for us, if not for God. To attempt to reconcile these two utterly different, some would say mutually exclusive, alternatives—God's foreknowledge and our present freedom to choose—would appear to most people futile; but they seem to present us with the choice of either being puppets in the hand of God or agents independent of Him. Pelagius would maintain that God has conceded us an element of free choice in this world. Augustine would deny that these alternatives are mutually exclusive, and it is easy

14. *Conf.* 11,13,15–14,17. *CSEL* 33,290–302; cf. *civ.* 11,21. *CCL* 48,339–40.

15. T. A. Lacey, *Nature, Miracle and Sin: A Study of St. Augustine's Conception of the Natural Order* (London, 1916), 64. Lacey's verdict was endorsed by Edwyn Bevan, *Symbolism and Belief* (London,1938; Fontana Library ed., 1963), 73–110, esp. p. 86: "It is apparent that all this language has come into Christian theology from the Greek Neo-Platonic infiltration."

to find quotations in his writings which declare both God's omnipotence and human freedom of choice. In the end, however, for Augustine divine omnipotence triumphed, and he declared in 427: "In the solution of this question I indeed laboured in defence of the free choice of the human will, but the grace of God conquered, and I was finally able to understand, with full clarity, the meaning of the Apostle: *For who singles thee out? Or what hast thou that thou hast not received? But if thou hast received it, why dost thou boast as if thou hadst not received it?*" (1 Cor. 4:7).[16]

However, until about 394/5 Augustine continued to entertain belief in free choice, for at least some persons, even in fallen humanity. In his *Commentary on the Epistle to the Romans,* composed while still a presbyter, he enunciated a theology of the Fall which is commonly associated with his thought: belief in a universal sinfulness, from which no one is set free except by the grace of God; human inability to perform any good work without grace; and the absolute absence of merit in God's eyes in any individual; but Augustine also suggested that, while we are not elected to salvation by any divine foreknowledge of the works which we will later do, God may choose individuals by His foreknowledge of their future *faith.*

Since the Holy Spirit is not given except to believers (cf. Eph. 1:13),

> God does not choose us for the works which He Himself bestows when He gives us the Spirit, in order that we may perform good works through charity. Rather, He chooses faith. For unless anyone believes in [God] and continues to be willing to receive [grace], he cannot receive the gift of God—that is the Holy Spirit—through whom, with the charity *which is poured into our hearts* (Rom. 5:5), he is able to do good works. Therefore God does not choose anyone in His foreknowledge of the works that He will give, but in His foreknowledge of the individual's faith. Accordingly, God chooses as the individual to whom He will give the Holy Spirit, one who, He knew, would believe, so that by doing good works he would also obtain eternal life. For the Apostle

16. *Retr.* 2,1,[27/28],1: "In cuius quaestionis solutione laboratum est quidem pro libero arbitrio voluntatis humanae; sed vicit dei gratia; nec nisi ad illud potuit perveniri, ut liquidissima veritate dixisse intellegatur apostolus: *Quis enim te discernit? Quid autem habes quod non accepisti? Si autem accepisti, quid gloriaris quasi non acceperis?*" CCL 57,89–90. Tr. Bogan.

says: *It is the same God who works all things in everyone* (1 Cor. 12:6). It has never been said: "God believes all things in everyone." Therefore, that we believe is of us; but what we do well comes from Him who gives the Holy Spirit to those believing in Him.[17]

Faith, not works; but it is God's foreknowledge of our future faith which causes Him to bestow the grace by which we may do the good works. The power to believe, however, belongs to the individual: "that we believe is of us, but what we do well comes from Him to those believing in him." When Augustine came to write the *Retractations* in 427, he criticized this saying, not because it was erroneous in itself (in spite of everything, Augustine still wanted to insist that we have free choice of the will) but because before we will, God must prepare the will. We are free, therefore, only after the reception of God's grace, which enables us to be free. Grace is given to the faithful soul; but it is given that it may become faithful, not because it is already so.

It is to be noticed that the general theology of the *Commentary on the Epistle to the Romans* is already that which Augustine will maintain against the Pelagians. The one exception is his belief that grace may be given because of faith—precisely the issue on which he was to differ from the Semi-Pelagians of Marseilles thirty years later. In the *Retractations,* in discussing what he now considered to be a former error on his part, he wrote: "Up to this time I had not yet sought diligently enough or discovered what is the nature of the election to grace, concerning which the same Apostle says: *There is a remnant left selected out of grace* (cf. Rom. 11:5). This certainly is not grace, if any merits precede it."[18]

A year later, when replying to the enquiries of his old pastor Simplicianus, Ambrose's successor in the see of Milan, regarding certain Pauline passages, Augustine by his own account had an intellectual illumination comparable though not identical with that experienced at Milan in 386. In both cases the conversion was initiated by a Pauline text. At Milan it was Romans 13:13–14: *Not in dissipation and drunkenness, not in de-*

17. *Exp. Rom.* 52(60),9–13. *CSEL* 84,34–5.
18. *Retr.* 1,22[23],2. *CCL* 57,68–9. Tr. Bogan.

bauchery and lewdness, not in arguing and jealousy; but put on the Lord Jesus Christ and make no provision for the flesh or the gratificaion of its desires. At Hippo, it was 1 Corinthians 4:7: *For who singles you out? Or what have you that you did not receive? And if you received it, why do you boast as if you had not received it?* Both these Pauline quotations have become famous in the history of Augustine's religious development and both have been seen, in some measure, as epitomizing the nature of the decision which he was going to make; but can we regard them as being historically as decisive as Augustine's references imply? In the case of Romans 13:13–14, this may well have been a decisive text at a psychological moment;[19] but with 1 Corinthians 4:7 the matter is more complicated. Of the importance of the composition of the *Ad Simplicianum* in Augustine's intellectual career there can be no question—there is no doubt that 1 Corinthians 4:7 became a proof-text for him in later life;[20] but writing the *Ad Simplicianum* may well be understood, not as involving a "road to Damascus" conversion, altering Augustine's thought at a particular moment in time, but as the culmination of a process which had been in progress for several years. His entire writings against the Manichees, whether he was speaking of Adam's condition before the Fall or not, were a defense of human free choice. However, by the time that he came to write the third and final book of the *De Libero Arbitrio (Of Free Choice)* in 391–93, he had come to take a far more pessimistic view of the human condition than when he began the work in 388. His first citation of 1 Corinthians 4:7 comes in a sermon, *Enarratio in Ps. 3,* 3 in 394–95.[21] Here it is used as a pulpit exhortation against pride. About the same time it appears in Question 69,7 of the *De Diversis Quaestionibus octoginta-tribus,* which forms part of a collection put together in 395/6. Here, the theme is that, at the end of the age, God will be all in all and that none of those who cleave to Him will prefer anything of his own will against God's will. *What have you that you did not receive?*

19. It is significant that in the garden at Milan the Bible plays a rôle similar to the pagan divination by the *sortes virgilianae.*

20. See the list provided by Hombert, *Gloria Gratiae* (1996), 22–24.

21. Ibid., p. 22.

In the *Ad Simplicianum* the text is cited once in its entirety[22] and twice in part,[23] with reference to God having loved Jacob and hated Esau when they were both in the womb and had not done anything good or evil, or had faith. *I will have mercy on whom I will have mercy and I will have compassion in whom I have compassion* (Rom. 9:15). All humanity is under a common condemnation, and if God in His mercy elects to save some out of the mass of sinners, the rest, who are left to His justice, have no ground for complaint. *O man, who art thou that repliest against God?* (Rom. 9:20).

Augustine regarded the *Ad Simplicianum* as a statement of his mature theological opinion, referring to it during the Pelagian Controversy in *On the Predestination of the Saints,* 3,7 and 4,8 (428/429) and *The Gift of Perseverance,* 17,45 (429), where he quotes 1 Corinthians 4:7. In the *Retractations* I I,1 [28/29], he speaks as if it were St. Cyprian's *Three Books of Testimonies to Quirinus* III,4[24] which drew his attention to the significance of the Corinthians quotation. Furthermore, in *On the Predestination of the Saints,* 4,8, he states that it was God who solved for him the problem of free choice when he was writing to Simplicianus. This statement can be read as implying a sudden illumination; but it could also, and I think more plausibly, mean that the intensive study of Pauline writing undertaken by Augustine on the eve of his episcopal consecration and summed up in the *Ad Simplicianum* could be understood as a divine illumination, but not necessarily experienced at a particular instant. In the *Ad Simplicianum* every trace of human initiative, independent of God's prompting, is swept away. Left to itself the fallen human will avails only for evil, and this is just, because God is the creator of man.

If God hated Esau, who was a vessel made for dishonor, then in their case the same potter has made one vessel for honor [Jacob] and another for dishonor. How is it then, that *Thou hatest nothing that thou hast made?* (Wis. 11:25). The

22. *Ad Simp.* 1,2,9. *CCL* 44,34.

23. Ibid., 1,2,10: "Si ergo Iacob ideo credidit quia voluit, non ei Deus donavit fidem, sed eam sibi ipse volendo praestitit, et habuit aliquid quod non accepit"; 1,2,17: "nec ille cui [Deus] donat, debet de suis meritis gloriari . . . et ille non habet, nisi quod accepit." *CCL* 57,34; 44.

24. *Retr.* 2,1[27/28],1. *CCL* 57,90.

problem is resolved if we understand that God is the creator of all that is made, and that *every creature of God is good* (1 Tim. 4:4). Every man, then, inasmuch as he is human, is a creature, but not inasmuch as he is a sinner. God is the creator of the human body and soul. Neither of these is evil and neither of them does God hate. He hates nothing that He has made. Now the soul is superior to the body. God indeed is superior to body and soul alike, and being the artist and creator of both, He hates nothing in man but sin. Human sin is disorder and perversity, that is aversion from the creator and conversion to inferior created things. God, then, did not hate Esau as a man, but hated him as a sinner. . . . Why did God love Joseph? Was he not also a sinner? What He loved in him was not the fault, which He had blotted out, but the grace which He had given.[25]

We are all guilty before God, but some are saved by His mercy. Augustine could fairly claim that his whole anti-Pelagian theology had long since been expressed in the *Ad Simplicianum*. As he put it in a letter (*Ep.* 194,5,19) written to the future Pope Sixtus of Rome in 418/9: "When God crowns our merits He crowns nothing more than His own gifts"; and beside these words may be set those written about the same time in the letter (*Ep.* 190.3.12) to Optatus: "God by his creation has willed so many souls to be born who, He foreknew, would have no part in His grace."[26]

Agostino Trapè, in his study *Agostino. L'uomo, il pastore, il mystico* (1976; English trans.1986), did not agree with those who considered "Augustine's doctrinal synthesis on grace, and especially the part which deals with predestination [to be] a pessimistic and hopeless vision of reality,"[27] and Pierre-Marie Hombert, in his very learned study, has commended Trapè's book as presenting "without doubt the best presentation of Augustine, 'Doctor of Grace,' to this day."[28] In the light of Augustine's language it is difficult to agree with Trapè and Hombert. Dr. Isabel Bochet, in an admirable study, *Saint Augustin et le désir de Dieu,* whose approach to Augustine is essentially optimistic, emphasizing the importance of will

25. *Ad Simp.* 1,2,18. *CCL* 44,44–45.

26. *Ep.* 194,5,19; 190,3,12. *CSEL* 57,190; 146.

27. Agostino Trapè, *Saint Augustine: Man, Pastor, Mystic.* (New York, 1986), 210.

28. Hombert, *Gloria Gratiae*, p. 7.

(voluntas) in Augustine's spirituality, took care to choose her texts from writings of his middle period. "The writings of Augustine's youth have already been the subject of a number of works. As for the last works, they most commonly have a polemical character and represent a certain hardening of his thought."[29] In fact, Augustine's earlier anti-Pelagian writings are deliberately restrained in their language: he regarded the Pelagians as brothers to be reasoned with rather than as heretics to be pursued. His fear was that their emphasis on virtuous living, admirable in itself, might lead to spiritual pride, the head and fount of sin; but his fundamental conviction of God's omnipotence, which led him to deny that the text of 1 Timothy 2:4: *God will have all men to be saved,* could mean what it said, was unaffected. For Augustine, not all are saved, and without God's special grace they cannot hope to work out their salvation.

Energy and ink have been expended in discussing whether Augustine's predestinarian theology is the same as Calvin's. Technically they can be differentiated. Calvin's teaching is supralapsarian: from eternity, God has willed certain individuals to reprobation. Augustine, on the other hand, asserts that human condemnation is a consequence of the Fall, which God foreknew. In practice, the two theologies are effectively the same, except that Calvin, who admired Augustine, nevertheless recoiled, like many other theologians, from his belief in the necessary damnation of unbaptized infants.[30] There is, however, one important distinction between Augustine and later Calvinism: Augustine did not believe it possible to distinguish between the saved and the reprobate in this life. As long as we are in the body, no one can have that "assurance of salvation" which was to be found in certain Calvinist circles in the seventeenth and eighteenth centuries and which was, in the nineteenth, the subject of James Hogg's anti-predestinarian novel, *The Confessions of a Justified Sin-*

29. Bochet, (Paris 1982), p. 17.

30. Calvin, *Institutio* 4,15,20: "I answer that this teaching is madness. In telling us that He will be the God of our seed after us, God declares that He adopts our children and keeps them as His before they are born." Calvin's position is founded on 1 Corinthians 7:14: *Else were your children unclean;* and Romans 11:23: *And if they do not persist in unbelief, they will be grafted in, for God is able to graft them in again.*

ner. Did Augustine ever maintain a belief in assurance in respect of himself? It has been suggested that his reference in *Confessions* X,35,56 to diabolic temptations "to seek some sign of God" implied that he wished to be assured of salvation.[31] There is, however, nothing decisive in the wording of this passage to justify such an interpretation. Augustine is discussing astrology and divination, and the "sign" would as well refer to general questioning regarding coming events as to Augustine's state in the eyes of God. It may be that the experiences of his career, which led first to baptism and then to ordination, would have persuaded Augustine to believe that "the son of his mother's tears" could surely not perish everlastingly; but this would not, in itself, imply any assurance of predestination. More than that it would be unwise to conjecture.

Augustine, then, realized the implications of the doctrine of creation from nothing: we exist and have life because God wills it and we are in His hands to dispose of as He decrees. Having mysteriously abused the freedom given to Adam at the creation and incurred mortal guilt, we are all deserving of damnation and have no reason to complain if God consigns us all to hell; but in His mercy God has chosen a remnant, to replace the angels who fell before the creation of the world, and we may hope to belong to it.

Nevertheless, even in the reprobate the image of God in the human soul has not been wholly erased by Adam's primal sin; some trace of our heavenly origin remains. Fallen man has "immortal longings" and is drawn to God by the very reason of his existence. Human beings desire

31. See John K. Ryan, *The Confessions of St. Augustine* (New York, 1960), 406, with reference to *conf.* 10,35,56: "Augustine was apparently subjected to severe temptations to seek some visible sign from God that he was assured of salvation." This was certainly not the case in 426/7. See *cor. et grat.* 13,40: "quis enim ex multitudine fidelium, quamdiu in hac mortalitate vivitur, in numero praedestinatorum se esse praesumeret?" and cf. Augustine's verdict in *civ.* 11,22: "Divine providence thus warns us not to indulge in silly complaints about the state of affairs, but to take pains to enquire what useful purposes are served by things. And when we fail to find the answer, either through deficiency of insight or of staying power, we should believe that the purpose is hidden from us, as it was in many cases where we had great difficulty in discovering it. There is a useful purpose in the obscurity of the purpose; it may serve to exercise our humility or to undermine our pride." Tr. Bettenson.

to be happy and so have an instinct for God, the source of all happiness, even though, without God's grace, they mistake their goal and find happiness in created things, good in themselves but evil if they distract the soul from pursuing its only true happiness in God. The fact that the capacity to enjoy God was never utterly destroyed by the Fall remained part of Augustine's theology throughout the Pelagian Controversy. In *The Spirit and the Letter,* written at the very beginning of the controversy, Augustine could write: "You must remember that the image of God in the human soul has not been so completely obliterated by the stain of earthly affections that no faint outlines of the original remain therein, and therefore it can rightly be said even in the ungodliness of its life to do or to hold some parts of the Law";[32] while in the twenty-second book of *The City of God,* composed in 426, he declared: "Man breeds like the beasts; and yet there is still the spark, as it were, of that reason, in virtue of which he was made in the image of God; that spark has not been utterly put out."[33] It is in this same chapter of *The City of God* that Augustine pronounces an encomium upon the human intellect and its achievements, only to add that this nature would not have fallen into its present spiritual wretchedness, "had it not been for the overwhelming gravity of that first sin committed by the first man, the father of the whole human race."[34]

Such, according to Augustine, is the greatness and misery of fallen humanity, rightly condemned yet still retaining traces of its heavenly origin. Fallen humanity deems itself to be free, but how can it be called free within the terms of Augustine's thinking? This will be the next subject for consideration.

32. *Sp. et litt.,* 28,48: "Verum tamen . . . non usque adeo in anima humana imago dei terrenorum affectuum labe detrita est, ut nulla in ea velut linamenta extrema remanserint." *CSEL* 60,202.

33. *Civ.* 22,24,2: "Ex quo enim homo in honore positus, postea quam deliquit, comparatus est pecoribus (Ps. 48:13 [49:12]) similiter generat; non in eo tamen penitus extincta est quaedam velut scintilla rationis, in qua factus est ad imaginem Dei." *CCL* 48,847.

34. Ibid., 3: ". . . huius tantae naturae conditor cum sit utique Deus verus et summus, ipso cuncta quae fecit administrante et summam potestatem summamque habente iustitiam, numquam profecto in has miserias decidisset, atque ex his, praeter eos solos qui liberabuntur, in aeternas esse itura, nisi nimis grande peccatum in homine primo, de quo caeteri exorti sunt, praecessisset." *CCL* 48,849.

CHAPTER 3

THE NATURE OF FREEDOM IN THE MIND OF AUGUSTINE

FREEDOM MAY BE UNDERSTOOD as the absence of constraint, the capacity to follow one's own desires and inclinations without hindrance. In the human animal, a being endowed with reasoning powers, freedom increases with maturity and is, indeed, a sign of maturity. A child, in its own interests, may be allowed freedom only to a limited degree, because it has only limited judgment. As the individual becomes an adult, more and more freedom may be accorded, and not only accorded but deemed desirable. A grown man or woman is expected to exercise free will, and not be continually turning to another person for authority to act. The evil of slavery is that it deprives the slave of freedom of choice and makes his actions dependent upon another's will. Admittedly, complete freedom of action, unrestrained by reason or charity, is the mark of the tyrant or the madman; but servitude, the state of being a slave, takes away an essential element of the human condition. To be truly human the individual needs a measure of free choice and individual responsibility.

The recognition of this necessity inspires a distinct variety of modern atheism.[1] When the public avowal of unbelief became permitted, if hardly welcomed, in Western Europe in the eighteenth century, athe-

1. See Patrick Masterson, *Atheism and Alienation* (London: Pelican Books, 1973), and Marcel Neusch, *The Sources of Modern Atheism*, trans. Matthew J. O'Connell (New York/Ramsey, N.J., 1982). Also James Thrower's article in *The Oxford Companion to Christian Thought* (Oxford, 2000), 49–51.

ist thinkers were primarily concerned to repudiate any ultimate dualism of matter and spirit, such as had been assumed in the philosophy of Descartes and his disciples. Science, and particularly the system expounded by Isaac Newton, could be used to make matter the basis of spirit, and not spirit the basis of matter. The reply of the astronomer Laplace, when asked by Napoleon about the place of God in his *System of the World,* is well known: "Sire, I have not had need of this hypothesis." This type of atheism, based upon scientific discovery, continues, and can today be morally reinforced by reference to the many apparent imperfections of the world as we know it: "How can I be expected to believe in a god who allows the anopheles mosquito to spread malaria, with its horrible consequences for human beings?"

There is, however, another type of atheism, which attacks belief in God not simply because it is mistaken, but because it is held to prevent the human race from realizing its full potentialities. This type looks back to Ludwig Feuerbach (1804–72), who saw the idea of God as a projection by man of his own best qualities. In denying God, Feuerbach claimed to be emancipating man. In place of a fantastic heavenly state, he affirmed relations between real men. Karl Marx (1818–83), encouraged by the writings of Feuerbach, held that the rejection of religion must be total: man alone is the only absolute. Meanwhile, perhaps borrowing an idea from the Christian writer Friedrich von Hardenberg (Novalis) (1772–1801), Marx saw religion as "the opiate of the people." "The abolition of religion as the *illusory* happiness of the people is required for their *real* happiness. The demand to give up the illusions about its condition is *the demand to give up a condition which needs illusions.*"[2] Human happiness is to

2. Marx, *Contribution to the Critique of Hegel's Philosophy of Right,* quoted by Neusch, *Sources of Modern Athiesm,* p. 67. Novalis was not speaking of the proletariat but of the Philistine: "Philister leben nur ein Altagsleben. . . . Ihr sogennante Religion wirkt bloss wie ein Opiat: reizend, betäubend, Schmerzen und Schwäche stillend" (*Blütenstaub* [1798]). Charles Kingsley is credited with writing: "We have used the Bible as if it were a mere special constable's handbook, an opium dose for keeping beasts of burden patient, while they were being overloaded" (G. D. H. Cole and Raymond Postgate, *The Common People,* 2nd ed. [1938], 322, with comment: ". . . so sending on its travels a phrase which was to end up on the walls of the Red Square in Moscow in 1917"). The long-enduring

be found in the real world of social relations, not in the imagined world of religion. Nietzsche (1844–1900) notoriously proclaimed the death of God: God had to die because human beings had grown weary of him and wanted to live in freedom. Sigmund Freud (1856–1940) saw religion as a collective neurosis, an illusion without a future.

It would be possible to continue this catalogue of philosophical atheists to include more recent writers like Jean-Paul Sartre and Ernst Bloch, but their message is clear: "the existence of God is incompatible with an affirmation of the reality of human freedom."[3] This is a thesis which Augustine would have utterly rejected, and not simply because of being a Christian, but for philosophical reasons as well. So far as I am aware, Augustine never in his life questioned the existence of God. This was characteristic of his age, for the last centuries of the Western Roman Empire were not, like the last century of the Roman Republic, an age of skepticism, but rather of piety, some of it of a very superstitious character. At Milan in 386, just before his reading of the Neoplatonists, Augustine was attracted by Epicurean hedonism, but was unable to rid himself of belief in the immortality of the soul and of the consequences after death of our actions committed in the flesh.[4] Accordingly the biblical doctrine of man's absolute dependence upon God, his creator, went unquestioned by Augustine, for *in him we live and move and have our being* (Acts 17:28). We have no independent existence and to seek for it, as Adam did in Eden, is not only to commit the capital sin of pride, but to act in a self-contradictory fashion.

There was, however, a philosophical consideration which in itself would have prevented Augustine from entertaining any thought of an existence independent of God: the platonic concept of participation *(metoche, metousia)*. The notion underlying this conception is one of *sharing*, and it was used to describe the relation between an individual exist-

dislike of atheism finds expression in the London *Courier*'s announcement of the death of Shelley of 5 August 1822: "Shelley, the writer of some infidel poetry, has been drowned; *now* he knows whether there is a God or no."

3. Masterson, *Atheism and Alienation*, p. 137.

4. *Conf.* 6,16,26. *CSEL* 33,139.

ing thing and the archetype from which it derives the form of its being. Augustine describes this relationship in Question 46 of *De Diversis Quaestionibus octoginta-tribus:*

> Ideas are certain primary forms or stable and unchanging causes *(rationes)* of things contained in the divine intelligence, which are themselves unformed and on this account are eternal and exist in the same mode of being; and since they themselves neither come into being nor perish, everything which *may* come into being and perish, or which *does* come into being and perishes, is said to be formed after them.[5]

It follows that all created things exist only by participating in God, and if they cease to participate they perish and pass out of existence. Man enjoys a special relationship, because he is in *the image and likeness of God.* Because of this, he can participate not only in his creator but in the divine Wisdom. There are degrees of participation in the divine by created things. A lifeless thing participates only by having being; a living being—plant or animal—participates to a higher degree; but to participate in the highest measure, so far as it is given to a created being to participate in its creator, it is necessary to be made in the image of God, as Adam was.[6] Because of the Fall, Adam's descendants have fallen away from God, the source of spiritual heat and light, have become cold and darkened, and only become warm again and enlightened by returning to the sole source of warmth and illumination.[7]

5. *Div. quaest. LXXXIII,* q. 46,2. *CCL* 44A,71.

6. Ibid., q. 51,2: "Multis enim modis dici res possunt similes deo: aliae secundum virtutem et sapientiam factae, quia in ipso est virtus et sapientia non facta; aliae in quantum solum vivunt, quia ille summe et primitus vivit; aliae in quantum sunt, quia ille et summe et primitus est. Et ideo quae tantummodo sunt, nec tamen vivunt aut sapiunt, non perfecte, sed exigue sunt ad similitudinem eius, quia et ipsa bona sunt in ordine suo, cum sit ille super omnia bonus, a quo omnia bona procedunt. Omnia vero quae vivunt et non sapiunt, paulo amplius participant similitudinem. Quod enim vivit etiam est: non autem quidquid est etiam vivit. Iam porro quae sapiunt, ita illi similitudini sunt proxima, ut in creaturis nihil sit propinquius. Quod enim participat sapientiae et vivit et est: quod autem vivit necesse est ut sit, non necesse est ut sapiat. Quare cum homo possit particeps esse sapientiae secundum interiorem hominem, secundum ipsum ita est ad imaginem, ut nulla natura interposita formetur; et ideo nihil sit Deo coniunctius. Et sapit enim et vivit et est: qua creatura nihil est melius." *CCL* 44A,79–80.

7. *En. Ps. 103, serm.* 4,2. *CCL* 40,1522.

No nature can be depraved by vice except such as is made out of nothing. Its *nature* derives from the fact that it was made by God, but its *fall* derives from the fact that it was made out of nothing. Man did not fall to the extent that he became nothing at all; but by stooping to follow his own inclination *(inclinatus ad se ipsum)*, he became less than he was when he clung to God, who is Being in the highest degree. When man abandoned God and lived to himself to do his own pleasure, he did not become nothing, but approached nothingness.[8]

For Augustine, then, to turn away from God to pursue one's own ends is not freedom but self-diminution, which can only be remedied by returning to God; but fallen man, being made from nothing, has no power of himself to attempt such a return. Only God can do this, and He has chosen to do this by Himself becoming man and sharing human nature to bring that nature, fully restored, to Himself.

God, being made a righteous man, has interceded with God for man who is a sinner; for though there is no harmony between the sinner and the righteous, there is harmony between man and man. Therefore, joining to us the likeness *(similitudinem)* of His humanity, He took away the unlikeness *(dissimilitudinem)* of our iniquity, and having been made a partaker *(particeps)* of our mortality, made us partakers *(participes)* of His divinity.[9]

For Augustine, rebellion against God cannot improve our human status but only diminish it, because we are dependent upon Him for our being and our well-being. Thus, to seek freedom by rebelling against God is not only futile but suicidal. There can be no liberty in rebellion, but only self-destruction.

There is, however, another consideration in the discussion of freedom, namely happiness. Modern atheists have argued that religious belief is an illusory hope in a non-existent future state, which will compensate for the wretchedness of the real world in which we currently live. What is needed, they claim, is an alteration of the present world,

8. *Civ.* 14,13. *CCL* 48,434. Tr. Wand.

9. *Trin.* 4,2,4: "Deus itaque factus homo iustus intercessit Deo pro homine peccatore. Non enim congruit peccator iusto, sed congruit homini homo. Adiungens ergo nobis similitudinem humanitatis suae, abstulit dissimilitudinem iniquitatis nostrae, et factus particeps mortalitatis nostrae, fecit nos participes divinitatis suae." *CCL* 50,164; cf. 13,9,12. *CCL* 50,398–9.

in which true happiness is possible, and this can only be accomplished if humanity is liberated from the illusion of theism, which discourages efforts to create a better society and a happier world.

Augustine, on principle, rejects such a view: religious hope is not an illusion but prepares us for the true happiness which the elect will enjoy only after death. But what is happiness? We know when we have it subjectively, and even more perhaps, we know when we are *not* happy; but how are we to define it? Augustine was always convinced that human beings not only desired to be happy, but that this was a natural and proper desire for which man had been created. In his early dialogue *On the Happy Life,*[10] composed at Cassiciacum in 386, he asked whether happiness was satisfied desire, but in a fallen world this leaves us with the problem of the nature of the desire. Is a contented pig preferable to a discontented Socrates? And is the man who has desired and achieved an evil end truly happy? Augustine had experienced the desire for false happiness at Milan before his conversion, when he was hoping for a successful career. "I was hankering after honors, wealth, and marriage, but You [God] were laughing at me. Very bitter were the frustrations I endured in chasing my desires, but all the greater was Your kindness in being less and less prepared to let anything other than Yourself grow sweet in me."[11] The sight of a drunken beggar, who had been temporarily happy in his cups while Augustine was full of anxieties, showed Augustine the vanity of his ambition; yet, on reflection, Augustine suspected that he would not have wanted to change places with the beggar.

Nevertheless, "Let them leave me in peace," was his later verdict,

> who would argue: "It makes a difference what a person is happy about. That beggar enjoyed his wine, you sought to bask in glory." What kind of glory was that, Lord? None that was to be found in You [cf. 1 Cor. 1:31]; for just as his was no true joy, so mine was no true glory, and it overturned my mind the more. The beggar would sleep off his intoxication that same night, whereas I slept with mine and got up again, and would sleep and rise with it again . . . how many days![12]

10. *Beata v.* 1,10. *CCL* 29,70.
11. *Conf.* 6,6,9. *CSEL* 33,122.
12. *Conf.* 6,6,10. *CSEL* 33,123.

The happiness kindled by the praise of others continued to affect Augustine (as it does most people) as a Christian bishop. In Book X of *The Confessions,*[13] composed after his ordination, he admitted his pleasure in the praise of others; but this is at best an uncertain happiness, transitory and dependent upon circumstances for its enjoyment. But more: for Augustine the love of praise is itself a vice and not a virtue, though it may hold other vices in check.[14] It may inspire men to act virtuously, but for a wrong reason. To practice virtue for the love of praise, and not for its own sake, is to prostitute virtue.[15] Thus the heroes who built up the Roman Empire could claim no merit in the eyes of God. Augustine's bitter judgment upon them in *The City of God* is well known. "They have no reason to complain of the justice of God, the supreme and true. *They have received their reward in full*"—and now, of course, they are no longer happy![16]

Augustine's reflections on the nature of happiness before his conversion no doubt explain the discussion at Cassiciacum beginning on his birthday, 13 November 386, published as *On the Happy Life.* Assuming that this dialogue embodies the essence of the deliberations and was not composed by Augustine, as some suppose, it would appear that his mother, Monica, played a considerable part in the discussion and earned applause for her contributions. When Augustine suggested that an individual who possessed what he wanted could be called happy, she commented that only someone who desired and wished for good things was happy; if he wanted evil things, he was wretched—a remark which caused her son to say that she had "gained the stronghold of philosophy,"[17] since she had unconsciously echoed the views of Cicero in the *Hortensius:* the worst wretchedness is to desire what is wrong. The meeting agreed that only those things which are enduring can give happi-

13. Ibid., 10,37,61. *CSEL* 33,273.

14. *Civ.* 5,17. *CCL* 47,150.

15. Ibid., 5,20–21. *CCL* 47,156–8.

16. Ibid., 5,15. *CCL* 47,149. See G. Bonner, "*Perceperunt mercedem suam.* The Background and Theological Implications of *De Civitate Dei* V,15," *Studia Patristica* 18, 4 (1990): 3–7.

17. *Beata v.* 2,10. *CCL* 29,70.

ness[18] and that no one can be happy through the possession of transitory goods, because he suffers from the fear of losing them. Here again Monica intervened: happiness lies, not in the possession of good things but in the state of mind of the possessor, a statement which leads Augustine to conclude that whoever possesses God is happy.[19] But to possess God can only be on His terms: a virtuous life; obedience to His will; and freedom from the spirit of impurity, either in the sense of being demonically possessed or being defiled by vices and sins.[20] It is not, however, enough to live righteously: to possess God, one must also first seek Him,[21] for as Monica points out, everyone, in one sense, as God's creation, already has God; but the individual who lives righteously has a favorable *(propitius)* God, while the sinner has an unfavorable one.[22] The conclusion of the discussion, summed up by Augustine at the end of the second day, is that everyone is already happy who has found and possesses a favorable God; that not everyone is already happy who is still seeking God, even though he possesses a benevolent God; while the sinner is not only unhappy, he does not even possess a favorable God.[23] On the third and final day of the discussion it was agreed that to be without wisdom is to be in want *(egestas)*,[24] and that wisdom is the wisdom of God, that is, the Son of God,[25] the Truth, who brings us to the Supreme Measure *(summus modus)*, the Father.

> Whoever, therefore, comes to the Supreme Measure [which is God], through the truth, is happy. This means to have God within the soul, that is, to enjoy God. Other things do not have God, although they are possessed by God.[26]

Here, the approach has changed. Unhappiness is defined as want, and want is due to *stultitia*, foolishness.[27] The cure for foolishness is wisdom, *sapientia*, the measure of the soul *(modus animi)*, through which the soul

18. Ibid., 2,11. *CCL* 29,71–72.
19. Ibid., 2,12. *CCL* 29,72.
20. Ibid., 3,18. *CCL* 29,75.
21. Ibid., 3,19. *CCL* 29,76.
22. Ibid., 3,19–20. *CCL* 29,76–77.
23. Ibid., 3,21. *CCL* 29,77.
24. Ibid., 4,29. *CCL* 29,81.
25. Ibid., 4,34. *CCL* 29,84.
26. Ibid., 4,35: "Quisquis igitur ad summum modum per veritatem venerit, beatus est." *CCL* 29,84.
27. Cf. 4,32. *CCL* 29,83.

is kept in balance, so that it neither runs over into excess nor falls short of its true fullness. If it runs over, it runs over

> into luxuries, despotism, pride, and similar things, through which the souls of immoderate and wretched men think that they can attain joy and power. But if the soul is constrained by squalid meanness, fears, grief, and covetousness, and similar things, whatever they may be, wretched men confess themselves to be wretched.[28]

Hitherto, one might say, Augustine's reasoning has been of a Platonic and Stoic character, but now he becomes specifically Christian. The wisdom by which the soul's ignorance is cured and made happy is the Wisdom of God. We need to remember God, to seek Him, and thirst for Him tirelessly.[29]

Augustine's philosophy, then, has no place for independence from God. On the contrary, it is only by possessing, and by being possessed by, God that the human soul can realize itself. Furthermore, the consequences of the soul's attempting to be its own master are that it becomes a slave to material things by enjoying them instead of God, or by agonizing in the fear of losing them. Throughout his early career Augustine had had experience of this. At Milan he had admitted the appeal of an Epicurean materialist philosophy,[30] provided that one did not believe in any survival after death, as he did. He had been haunted by the will to a personal success,[31] without any consideration of its moral implications, though with belief in the influence of the stars upon human life and actions,[32] although he declined to enlist the help of magical rites to advance his interests. He subsequently admitted the power of lust and ambition to fetter his free will, and likened it to a chain;[33] but later he recognized that he had entertained a false conviction of his own capability, which made him unwilling to look to God for healing.[34]

What is to be remarked is that for Augustine the alienation from God

28. Ibid., 4,33. *CCL* 29,84.
29. Ibid., 4,35. *CCL* 29,84–5.
30. *Conf.* 6,16,26. *CSEL* 33,139.
31. Ibid., 6,6,9. *CSEL* 33,122.
32. Ibid., 4,2,3–3,6; 7,6,8. *CSEL* 33,64–68; 148–52.
33. Ibid., 6,12,21; 8,5,10; 11,25. *CSEL* 33,135;178;191.
34. Ibid., 6,11,20. *CSEL* 33,134.

which he experienced at Milan previous to his conversion did not provide any sense of freedom, and that the distractions from God, caused by ambition and sexual desire, did not, in his case, offer any real satisfaction. Nevertheless, they did bring home the weakness of his will to command his mind and his body and help to explain the prayer in *The Confessions* which so offended Pelagius: "You command chastity and continence. Give what you command and command what you will."[35] It might be said that this petition represents Augustine's picture of the relationship between himself and his Maker and is the answer to his struggles for chastity on the eve of his conversion, described at the end of Book IX of *The Confessions,* when Augustine wished to be chaste and yet was unable to make up his mind. God's grace overtook him in the garden of Milan and the incident is enshrined in this brief and very personal prayer.

The prayer, "Give what you command," expresses Augustine's need for God, not felt by modern atheists, and therefore not understood by them. *My soul is athirst for God, yea, even for the living God; when shall I come to appear before the presence of God?* (Ps. 42:2). For those who have such a thirst, everything else, even things good in themselves because they are God's creation, never have the value which others put upon them. In Augustine's case, this goes far to explain his attitude to the created world. As a lover of beauty he was not insensitive to nature, though as a Christian Platonist he would hold that, because of its transitory nature, it was the lowest manifestation of beauty—*Whatever fades but fading pleasure brings*—and his thirst was for the unchanging and eternal, for the God who does not change and who changes His elect by participation in His eternal deity, "not to temporal happiness but by adoption to eternal life, which alone is happy."[36]

35. Ibid., 10,29,40. *CSEL* 33,256; *dono pers.* 20,53. *PL* 45,1026.

36. *Ep.* 140,36,82: "non ad temporalem felicitatem, sed ad vitae aeternae, quae sola beata est, adoptionem." *CSEL* 44,230. See Robert J. O'Connell, *Art and the Christian Intelligence in St. Augustine* (Oxford: Basil Blackwell, 1978), esp. pp. 87–90; G. Bonner, "The Significance of Augustine's *De Gratia Novi Testamenti,*" *Augustiniana* (1990): 531–59, reprinted in *Church and Faith in the Patristic Tradition* (Aldershot: Variorum, 1996), no. IV; "Augustine's Thoughts on This World and Hope for the Next," *The Princeton Seminary Bulletin,* supplementary issue no. 3 (1994): 85–103.

This attitude may be set against Augustine's emphasis, at the end of his life, upon the helplessness of the individual without the grace of God. A lover does not ask if he is free; he loves, and that is enough. As a dogmatic theologian Augustine discussed the relations between grace, predestination, and freedom, and came to conclusions which shock many readers today. As a teacher of spirituality and of the ascent of the mind to God, he took for granted a desire for God naturally existing in the human soul by reason of its creation in *the image and likeness of God,* and in *The Confessions* used his own experiences as a case history of such a seeking and finding. To what extent are his descriptions of his Platonic ecstasies at Milan before his conversion and of the Vision of Ostia experienced with Monica just before her death to be regarded as accounts of genuine mystical experiences? Some dogmatic theologians, while accepting the Vision of Ostia, have declined to regard the experiences at Milan as truly mystical, because they occurred while Augustine was still unbaptized. The historian, looking at the three descriptions,[37] will find in all three a strongly Platonic character, though the first is a vision of light; the second an ascent of the mind, in what may also be read as a theory of epistemology; and the third a progressive silencing of the created world in order that God may speak out of the silence—though he may well also reflect that *the spirit blows where it wills* (John 3:8) and that it is unwise to seek to limit the operations of God's grace to dogmatic formulations. The point is that Augustine, in all these experiences, had attempted to raise his mind to God, and believed himself, at least for an instant, to have touched the Supreme Reality, "Him Who Is," "the Selfsame." Did Augustine feel that what he experienced at Ostia was an intimation, however brief, of the eternal joys of heaven? It would appear that he did.

If this could last, and all other visions, so far inferior, be taken away, and this sight alone ravish him who saw it, and engulf him and hide him away, kept for inward joys, so that this moment of knowledge, this passing moment of

37. *Conf.* 7,10,16; 7,17,23; 9,10,25. *CSEL* 33,157; 161–3; 217–8. See Paul Henry, *La Vision d'Ostie* (Paris, 1938); English trans., *The Path to Transcendence* (Pittsburgh, 1981).

knowledge that left aching for more should there be life eternal, would not *Enter into the joy of your Lord* (Matt. 25:21) be this, and this alone?[38]

One can therefore read Augustine's account of the ecstasies of Milan and Ostia as descriptions of the attempts of one human soul, under the impulse of God, whether consciously experienced or not, to raise itself to God, its creator, guardian and guide, and true end. It is significant that when Augustine came to record the episodes at Milan in *The Confessions,* he described them as having pointed him the way to Christianity.

And I sought for a way to gain the strength necessary to enjoy You, but I did not find it until I embraced the Mediator between God and mankind, the man Christ Jesus, who is God over all things and blessed for ever. Not yet had I embraced Him, calling out and saying: *I am the Way and the Truth and the Life* (John 14:6)[39]

The conception of Jesus Christ, the God-man, who is the Mediator between God and man, is at the heart of Augustine's theology. He does not use the sort of devotional language which has become familiar to Western Christians since the Middle Ages, with its devotion to the self-humiliated Divine Humanity; but for him the Incarnation is God's plan, not only to redeem the world, but to unite human beings in a closer bond than that which linked Adam to God before the Fall, by associating Godhead and Manhood in the person of Jesus Christ. Christ is one Person in two Natures, and the two Natures are indissolubly bound in His one Person, while remaining wholly distinct in themselves. Accordingly, Augustine can declare in the *Enchiridion ad Laurentium,* the nearest thing to a work of dogmatic theology which he ever composed:

So Jesus Christ, the Son of God, is God and man: God before all worlds, man in our world; God because He is the Word of God, *for the Word was God* (John 1:1), and man because a rational soul and flesh were joined to the Word in one Person. Therefore, insofar as He is God, He and the Father are one; and insofar as He is man, the Father is greater than He. But since He is the only Son of God, by

38. *Conf.* 9,10,25. Tr. Boulding. See Andrew Louth, *The Origins of the Christian Mystical Tradition* (Oxford, 1981), 136ff.

39. *Conf.* 7,18,24. *CSEL* 33,163. Tr. Boulding.

nature and not by grace, He became also the Son of Man, that He might also be full of grace. He, one and the same, is both, one Christ from both natures.[40]

Augustine is in the patristic tradition in understanding that the purpose of the Incarnation was the salvation of the human race. No more appropriate way could have been found to release humanity from the power of Satan than for God to take human form and, by suffering an unjust death at the hands of the devil, take away the devil's power, because he had abused that power by putting to death a sinless man, over whom he had no authority. The arch-deceiver was himself deceived. This notion enjoyed much popularity with the Fathers, though it may not appeal to our own age which, while being prepared to give the devil his due and rather more, perhaps, than his due, does not care to think of God acting as a clever defending lawyer, who traps the accuser into a false admission. More significant theologically, we may feel, is that the Incarnation is, for Augustine, a supreme example of divine humility. By taking human flesh and dying, Christ put to shame the fallen angels, who deemed themselves superior to human beings by not having material bodies.[41] But more than this: in the Incarnation "God Himself, the blessed God, who is the giver of blessedness, became partaker of our human nature, and thus offered us a shortcut *(compendium praebuit)* to participation in

40. *Ench.* 10,35: "Proinde Christus Iesus dei filius est et deus et homo: deus ante omnia saecula, homo in nostro saeculo; deus, quia dei Verbum: *deus enim erat Verbum* (Ioh. 1:1); homo autem, quia in unitatem personae accessit Verbo anima rationalis et caro. Quocirco, in quantum deus est, ipse et pater unum sunt (Ioh.10:30); in quantum autem homo est, pater maior est illo (Ioh.14:28). Cum enim esset unicus dei filius, non gratia sed natura, ut esset etiam plenus gratia, factus est et hominis filius; idemque ipse utrumque, ex utroque unus Christus." *CCL* 46,69.

41. *Trin.* 13,17,22: "Sunt et alia multa quae in Christi incarnatione, quae superbis displicet, salubriter intuenda et cogitanda sunt. Quorum est unum quod demonstratum est homini, quem locum haberet in rebus quas condidit deus quandoquidem sic deo coniungi potuit humana natura, ut ex duabus substantiis fieret una persona ac per hoc iam ex tribus, deo, anima et carne; ut superbi illi maligni spiritus qui se ad decipiendum quasi ad adiuvandum medios interponunt, non ideo se audeant homini praeponere quia non habunt carnem; et maxime quia et mori in eadem carne dignatus est filius dei ne ideo illi tamquam deos se coli persuadeant, quia videntur esse immortales." *CCL* 50A,412.

His own divine nature."[42] (When Augustine speaks of a "shortcut," I suspect that he opposes the action of the Incarnation to the elaborate magical rites which attracted later Platonists like Iamblichus.) However, the point to notice is the word "participation." Everything which exists partakes in some degree of God. In the case of man, made in God's image, the participation is of a special nature. But Augustine goes further. Because of Christ's two-natured Person, God has Himself chosen to participate in His own creation, humanity, and it is by participation in Christ that human nature may, in some measure, participate in the divine, even though it is itself created and remains created.

This higher participation is called deification *(theosis, theopoiesis)* and is a conception not infrequently to be found in the Greek Fathers, its most famous formulation probably being the lapidary sentence of St. Athanasius in the *De Incarnatione:* "He was made human that we might be made divine,"[43] which was anticipated by St. Irenaeus in *Adversus Haereses*[44] and paralleled by Augustine in his Sermon 192: *"Deos facturus qui homines erant, homo factus est qui Deus erat"*—"To make gods those who were men, He was made man who was God."[45] This language does not mean that redeemed humanity is made equal with God, but that it is brought into a special relationship by adoption. Augustine explains his understanding of the Pauline term *huiothesia* in his comment on Galatians 4:5:

> *That we should receive the adoption,* says the Apostle, *of sons.* He says *adoption (adoptio)* for this reason, that we may clearly understand the Son of God to be the only Son, for we are sons of God by the favor and ennobling *(dignatione)* of His mercy; but He is by nature the Son, who is what the Father is. Nor does the Apostle say: *that we might accept* but *that we might receive,* to signify that we had lost this sonship in Adam, through whom we are mortals. . . . Hence we receive adoption because Christ, the Only-Begotten, has not disdained to participate in

42. *Civ.* 9,15,2: "factus particeps humanitatis nostrae compendium praebuit participandae divinitatis suae." *CCL* 47,263.

43. Athanasius, *De Incarnatione* 54,3. *PG* 25, 192B.

44. Irenaeus, *Adv. Haereses* 5, *Praef.:* ". . . Verbum Dei, Iesum Christum Dominum nostrum, qui propter immensam suam dilectionem factus est quod sumus nos, uti nos perficeret esse quod est ipse." *SC* 153,13.

45. Aug., *serm.* 192,i,1. *PL* 38,1012.

our nature, having been made out of woman, that He should not only be the Only-Begotten where He has no brethren, but also be made the First-Begotten of many brethren.[46]

Augustine amplifies this understanding of adoption as the cause of deification in *De Trinitate* IV:

We are not divine by nature, we are human, and by sin we are not righteous. So God, being made a righteous man, interceded with God for sinful men and women. The sinner has nothing in common with the Righteous One, but man has humanity in common with a man. Therefore joining to us the likeness of His humanity, He took away the unlikeness of our iniquity; and being made a sharer *(particeps)* of our mortality, He made us sharers of His divinity.[47]

Whence did Augustine derive his theology of deification? It could be from Irenaeus, whose *Adversus Haereses* had been translated into Latin by 421, when Augustine himself quotes from it (*c.Iul.* 1,3,5), and whose teaching may well have been familiar in the West even before the translation. But Irenaeus apart, the Roman presbyter and antipope Novatian (mid-third century), in his treatise *On the Trinity,*[48] speaks of Christ as bestowing divinity upon humanity through immortality. Whatever his source may be, Augustine's language when he speaks of deification contrasts so remarkably with the tone of his later anti-Pelagian writings as to persuade some scholars who have not read him widely that deification is the doctrine of Eastern Christendom, while justification is that of the West. This view is simply wrong; but the contrast in Augustine's

46. *Ep. Gal. exp.* 30,6: "Vt adoptionem, inquit, filiorum recipiamus. *Adoptionem* propterea dicit ut distincte intelligamus unicum dei filium. Nos enim beneficio et dignatione misericordiae eius filii dei sumus, ille natura est filius, qui hoc est quod pater." *CSEL* 84,96.

47. *Trin.* 4,2,4. *CCL* 50,164.

48. Novatian, *trin.*,15,87: "Si homo tantummodo Christus, quomodo ait: *si quis verbum meum servaverit, mortem non videbit in aeternum?* Mortem in aeternum non videre, quid aliud quam immortalitas est? Immortalitas autem divinitati socia est, quia et immortalitas divinitatis fructus est. Sed enim omnis homo mortalis est; immortalitas autem ex mortali non potest esse. Ergo ex Christo homine mortali immortalitas non potest nasci. *Sed qui verbum custodierit,* inquit, *meum, mortem non videbit in aeternum.* Ergo verbum Christi praestat immortalitatem, et per immortalitatem praestat divinitatem." Ed. Weyer (Düsseldorf, 1962), 108. See the note by Yorke Fausset in his edition (Cambridge, 1909), pp. lv–lxi.

modes of theologizing is impressive. One is tempted to suppose that the disjunction which he makes between the election of the saved and the reprobation of the lost enables Augustine to speak so movingly of the deification of the minority and to ignore the fate of the vast majority with the same callous detachment which he shows when talking in the *Enchiridion* of the bodies of the reprobate when they rise for condemnation at the Last Judgment:

> Surely there is no need to expend effort in inquiring whether they will rise with the defects and deformities of their bodies and whatever defective and deformed limbs they had formerly. Nor should we weary ourselves by considering their appearance or beauty, since their damnation will be certain and unending.[49]

Let us, however, here confine ourselves to the elect, who by God's grace have been called to that union with God which is called deification. In the opinion of Augustine, this is a process completed only by death:

> Our full adoption as sons will take place only *in the redemption* of our body. We now have the *first fruits of the spirit*, by which we are indeed made sons of God, but in other respects we are sons of God as saved and made new by hope. In the event, however, since we are not yet finally saved, we are therefore not yet fully made new nor yet sons of God, but children of this world. We therefore go forward to renovation and the righteous life through which we are sons of God and therefore wholly unable to sin, until the whole of us is changed, even that by which we are children of this age and are still able to sin.[50]

As long as we are in the flesh, we are still able to sin. Only after death shall we reach the happy condition in which sinning is impossible. Does this imply any loss of freedom by the redeemed? Obviously not, so far

49. *Ench.* 23,92. *CSEL* 46,98.

50. *Pecc. mer. et rem.* 2,8,10: "Adoptio ergo plena filiorum in redemptione fiet etiam corporis nostri. primitias itaque spiritus nunc habemus, unde iam filii dei reipsa facti sumus: in caeteris vero spe sicut salvi, sicut innovati, ita et filii dei; re autem ipsa quia nondum salvi, ideo nondum plane innovati nondum etiam filii dei, sed filii saeculi. proficimus ergo in renovationem iustamque vitam, per quod filii dei sumus, et per hoc peccare omnino non possumus, donec totum in hoc transmutetur, etiam illud quo adhuc filii saeculi sumus; per hoc enim et peccare adhuc possumus." *CSEL* 60,81.

as Augustine is concerned. If one is in love with God, as Augustine was, and desirous of loving Him still more, then the fear that we may sin is not freedom, but anxiety, one of the obstacles to happiness, and a liability from which we pray to be relieved. In heaven, says Augustine,

> . . . the fact that sin will not be able to delight the redeemed does not mean that they will have no free will. Indeed, the will will be the more free, since it is free from a delight in sin, and immovably fixed in the happiness of not sinning. For the first freedom of will given to man when he was created upright was the ability not to sin, though being capable of sinning, but the last freedom will be stronger, because it will bring the impossibility of sinning. Yet this too will be God's gift, not some quality of nature. For it is one thing to be God, another to be a partaker of God *(particeps Dei)*. For God by nature cannot sin, but he who partakes of God's nature receives the inability to sin as a gift from God. The inability to sin belongs to God's nature, while he who partakes of God's nature receives the impossibility of sinning as a gift from God.[51]

The Lover is not so much concerned with freedom as with cleaving to the Beloved. What we are to understand as Augustine's general conception of free will will be the theme of our fourth chapter.

51. *Civ.* 22,30,3: "Nec ideo liberum arbitrium non habebunt, quia peccata eos delectare non poterunt. Magis quippe erit liberum a delectatione peccandi usque ad delectationem non peccandi indeclinabilem liberatum. Nam primum liberum arbitrium, quod homini datum est, quando primum creatus est rectus, potuit non peccare, sed potuit et peccare: hoc autem novissimum, eo potentius erit, quo peccare non potuit; verum hoc quoque Dei munere, non suae possibilitate naturae. Aliud est enim esse Deum; aliud participem Dei. Deus natura peccare non potest; particeps vero Dei ab illo accipit, ut peccare non possit." *CCL* 48,863; cf. *cor. et grat.* 12,33. *PL* 44,936.

CHAPTER 4

FREEDOM AND RESPONSIBILITY

A PUPPET CANNOT BE HELD responsible for its actions, nor can a man who, by reason of mental incapacity, has no control over his will. To be fully human, one needs to possess a will and be able to command it. In everyday life we expect this of our fellows; indeed, if we could not, the fabric of any association would disintegrate. In secular society, the notion of punishment includes the expectation that the offender, remembering the correction which he has endured, will in the future take care to avoid the course of action which provoked it. In short, we assume that normal people have control over their actions and that those who fail to exercise their will are either abnormal or culpable. Conversely, those who exercise their will for the good of others, especially if it is to their own disadvantage, are seen as virtuous and exemplary. They choose to do right, and are honored for it, since they could have chosen otherwise.

Such an approach, based on common experience, was that of Pelagius and his supporters. Pelagius, in his analysis of what constituted a good action, identified three elements: possibility, volition, and action. We must be able to do it; we must will to do it; and we must then do it. Possibility comes from God, volition and action come from ourselves. Thus in every good action there is praise for both God and man. It is of God alone that man is able to perform a good work; but it is for man to will the good work and to perform it.[1] The essential element here, which distinguishes Pelagian from Augustinian psychology, lies in the

1. *Grat. Christ. et pecc. orig.* 1,3–4. *CSEL* 42,127; Jerome, *Dialogus* 1,28. *PL* 23,544.

will. For Augustine, to will requires the gift of grace for every individual action: God crowns His own gifts and not human merits. If human merit is from man himself, it is not from God.[2] For Pelagius, although man's power comes from God, he is left with his own initiative; he is, in Julian of Eclanum's famous phrase, "emancipated from God":[3] God endows him with the initiative to act rightly. The word "emancipated" has a legal flavor: it recalls the ceremony by which a Roman son, or a slave, was released from the absolute power of his father or owner. But emancipation did not confer complete independence on the recipient. He was still bound to his parent or former owner by moral ties.

The ferocity of the conflict between Augustine and the Pelagians can obscure the fact that their analyses of God's action upon the human soul are not as different as appear on the first view. We may ignore Harnack's charge that Pelagius's system was fundamentally "godless"[4]—Pelagius, no less than Augustine, believed that God was the source of all human power. He differed from the mature Augustine in assuming that God gives each individual a personal power of free decision in life, which can be used for a moral or immoral end. This belief lies behind Julian of Eclanum's definition of human freedom: "Freedom of choice, by which man is emancipated from God, exists in the possibility of giving way to sin or of abstaining from sin."[5] The difference between the Augustinian and Pelagian views of human choice was determined by their attitudes to Adam's primal sin and its effect upon his descendants. The Pelagians denied the existence of any transmission of Adam's guilt. Of Adam himself, they—or at least Julian—had no very high opinion. "Raw, inexperienced, rash, without experience of fear or example of virtue, he took the food whose sweetness and beauty had ensnared him at the suggestion of a woman."[6] Again, "Adam was made a rational animal, mortal, capable

2. *Grat. et lib. arb.* 6,15. *PL* 44, 890.

3. *Op. imp.* 1,78: "Libertas arbitrii, qua a Deo emancipatus homo est, in admittendi peccati et abstinendi a peccato possibilitate consistit." *CSEL* 85/1,93.

4. Adolf von Harnack, *Lehrbuch der Dogmengeschichte* (1910) 201. Bd 3, 6th ed. (Tübingen, 1960), 201: "Im tiefsten Grunde guttlos."

5. *Op. imp.* 1,78. *CSEL* 85/1,93.

6. Ibid., 6,23. *CSEL* 85/2,373–4.

of virtue and vice, who was able, from the possibility conceded to him, to observe God's laws or to transgress; or by his natural power of command to preserve the law of human society; and being free, he had the power to wish either alternative and in that is the sum of sin and righteousness."[7] This, however, was not the real point, which was psychological. For Julian, sin does not cause moral freedom to perish. "Free choice is as full after committing sin as it was before."[8] "We say that the state of human nature is not changed by sin but the quality of human merit, that is, even in sin there is the nature of free choice, by which a man is able to cease from sin, just as it allowed him to turn away from righteousness."[9]

The distinction between this view of human nature and Augustine's is determined by the doctrine of the Fall. For Augustine, Adam was created far superior to any of his human descendants as they have become through his sin, in which they all mysteriously participated when he disobeyed God's commandment, and this, in Augustine's mature theology, has left them incapable of performing any good action without the immediate prevenient grace of God. God must always intervene. Hence Augustine's fondness for the text of Proverbs 8:35 in the Septuagint version: *the will is prepared by God (praeparatur voluntas a Domino).*[10] We do indeed have free choice to do good and evil; but while the slave of sin is free to do evil, no one is free to do good, unless he has been set free by Christ who said: *If the Son of Man shall set you free, then you will be free indeed* (John 7:36). Up to 394, as we have seen, Augustine was prepared to admit that God might give grace to those whose future faith He foresaw—a view resembling that of the Semi-Pelagian theologians of Marseilles, against whom his final writings were directed; but from 395/7 onwards he had decided otherwise: free choice for good requires the gift of grace, not simply that bestowed in our creation, but a special grace,

7. Ibid., 1,79. *CSEL* 85/1,94.

8. Ibid., 1,91. *CSEL* 85/1,104.

9. Ibid., 1,96. *CSEL* 85/1,111.

10. *Grat. et lib. arb.* 6,32. *PL* 44,900; *cor. et grat.* 4,6. *PL* 44,919; *praed. sanct.*, 5,10. *PL* 44,968.

necessary for our fallen condition. This view the Pelagians rejected. We are given grace in our individual creation sufficient to enable us to exercise free choice, and if we choose to abuse that free choice by doing evil, we are not thereby enfeebled in the future for doing good.

This belief determined the Pelagian view of grace, so inadequate in Augustine's eyes. They saw grace, both before and after the cleansing of sins by the grace of baptism, as being a matter of illumination and precept—a view which explains the sternness of the Anonymous Sicilian author, often reckoned a Pelagian: sinners have no excuse for their sinning. It has been remarked that the weakness of Pelagian theology lay in the simplicity of the view it held of the human will. It made no allowance for the influence and power of continued bad habit. In practice the Pelagians came to recognize that long-continued wrongdoing did have an effect on the power to will; but human freedom of choice in the present life remained a fundamental assumption of their theology. Thus the Sicilian Anonymous, in his treatise *On the Possibility of Not Sinning,*[11] argued that if somebody is told that he need not sin, this will at least encourage him to try as hard as he can not to do so, with the result that he will sin less than if he is persuaded that sin is unavoidable.

The Pelagian view of human nature undoubtedly allows for human responsibility: if you sin, you go to hell. "In the day of judgment," said Pelagius, "there will be no pardon for the wicked and sinners, but they

11. Sicilian anon., *De Possibiltate Non Peccandi,* 3,2. *PLS* 1,1460. The identity of the so-called Sicilian Anonymous author is discussed by F. G. Nuvolone and A. Solignac, "Pélage et Pélagianisme," *Dictionnaire de spiritualité, ascétique, mystique, doctrine et histoire* 12B (1986), 2889–942 and by B. R. Rees, *The Letters of Pelagius and His Followers* (Woodbridge, 1991), 16–18. The names of Pelagius, Agricola, Fastidius, and the future Pope Sixtus III have been suggested. More recently Dáibhí Ó Cróinín, in an article "Who Was Palladius, 'First Bishop of the Irish'?" *Peritia* 15 (2001): 205–32, has argued very persuasively that he was identical with the bishop sent in 431 by Pope Celestine to "the Irish believing in Christ," mentioned by Prosper of Aquitaine, who presumably had reconciled himself with the newly defined order of things after the condemnation of Pelagianism. It should, however, be remembered that while denial of any transmission of Original Sin was a useful foundation for exhorting Christians to Christian living, it was not essential, and that harsh asceticism can be acceptable to traducianists, as the example of Jerome indicates.

will be burned in eternal fires."[12] Behind this uncompromising declaration was the conviction that human beings already, in this life, have the ability to refrain from sin, if they choose. To deny this was to accuse God of having imposed on humanity commands which it cannot fulfill, and so to ascribe to God iniquity and cruelty. To sin constitutes a deliberate act of defiance, which rightly brings punishment on the sinner. But punishment apart, recollection of sin will produce a terrible shame at the Last Judgment. In his treatise *On Bad Teachers,* the Sicilian Anonymous, an advocate of extreme asceticism, speaks of the fear of everlasting punishment, which should deter us from doing evil, but then goes on:

> But let us suppose, as some men would have it, that we have no need to fear any future punishment in torment, or to dread burning by any eternal fire, and that we are to believe that such promises were made only to frighten us. Surely the discomfiture that awaits us at the Judgement ought to be enough to arouse our fear? What agonies of shame we shall feel when, before God's very eyes and in the sight of all the heavenly powers surrounding Him in heaven, of the martyrs and the other saints standing by, the secrets of everyone of us will be revealed, and all the sins which we have committed in thought and in deed will be exposed, as if they were actually being done there on the spot and represented in the sight of all. . . . What feelings of shame and disgrace, I ask you, will then confound the hearts of those above all who were thought in men's judgement to be holier than the rest of mortals, when they are seen to be different from what they have appeared to men to be?[13]

The shame comes from hypocrisy, and the hypocrisy lies in pretending to have done what one was capable of doing but neglected to do when one was capable of doing it and had the responsibility to do it. For the Sicilian Anonymous, responsibility implies and demands the capacity to act.

Given his belief in the capacity of the human will to act, there was reason in Pelagius's assertion that in any good action there was praise for God and man alike. God, in the act of creation, had bestowed upon

12. Aug., *gest. Pel.* 3,9. *CSEL* 42,60; Jerome, *Dialogus* 1,28. *PL* 23,544; cf. *De Malis Doctoribus* 17,1. *PLS* 1,1447.

13. Sicilian anon., *De Malis Doct.* 24,2–3. *PLS* 1,1456. Tr. B. R. Rees, *The Letters of Pelagius and His Followers,* 251.

man some of the freedom that characterizes His own being, and that freedom is an essential part of human nature, which cannot be lost, even by repeated sinning. However much we sin, there remains in us an enduring element of goodness and a power to do good.

This doctrine, of course, harmonizes with Augustine's notion of evil as a privation of goodness: so long as man, or any other created being exists, he must be essentially good; to be wholly evil would be to cease to exist. As a being, fallen man remains, for Augustine, good; he was evil only because of a perverted will, and aversion from God, which had led first to the primeval rebellion of Satan and then to the fall of Adam, which remains a mark of fallen humanity.[14] It is this aversion which explains Augustine's saying in the fifth *Tractate on the Gospel of John* that "no one has anything of his own except lying and sin" *(nemo habet de suo nisi mendacium et peccatum).*[15] Taken at its face value, this declaration might seem to justify Julian of Eclanum's accusation that Augustine had never, at heart, ceased to be a Manichee—what pertains to human nature appears to be fundamentally evil. But Augustine's thought was more complex. He based his argument on John 8:44, referring to the devil: *when he speaks a lie, he speaks from what is his,* the point being that Christ is the Truth and the source of all truth; therefore a man cannot be truthful except from the Truth. Yet the devil is *the father of lies.* The lie cannot come from his Creator, who is the Truth, and can therefore only be ascribed to the devil himself who, though created good, has become evil through his self-perverted will, the will being for Augustine a *media vis,* a neutral force which becomes good or evil according to the willing of its possessor.[16] Once it has been perverted by an abuse of free will, it remains perverted, lacking the grace of God. Therefore "no one has anything of his own except lying and sin."

14. *Ench.* 8,23: "nequaquam dubitare debemus rerum quae ad nos pertinent bonarum causam non nisi bonitatem dei, malarum vero ab immutabili bono deficientem boni mutabilis voluntatem, prius angeli, hominis postea." *CCL* 46,63.

15. *Io. Ev. tr.* 5,1. *CCL* 36,40.

16. *Sp. et litt.* 33,58: "media vis est, quae vel intendi ad fidem, vel inclinari ad infidelitatem potest." *CSEL* 60,216.

It may therefore reasonably be maintained that the fundamental difference between Pelagian and Augustinian theology turns upon the notion of will. For the Pelagian, God has endowed, and continues to endow, every human being with free will and the capacity to exercise it. For Augustine, God endowed humanity, in the person of Adam, with free will and the capacity to exercise it; but this capacity was voluntarily lost through the Fall and is restored only through God's intervention. Consciously or not, the contrast between these theologies was dramatically depicted by Augustine in his account of Pelagius's reaction to Augustine's words: "Give what You command and command what You will," when he broke out furiously, declaring that he could not endure such sentiments. Pelagius's reaction attracts sympathy, because it reflects the assumption widely held by human beings and taken for granted in human society, that individuals have a control over their actions and are responsible for them—the man who will not, or cannot, exercise control has to be restrained, if necessary by force. Augustine accepted this assumption in practice, so far as human society was concerned—earthly society needed organization and law enforcement, if it were to function for the well-being of its inhabitants; but his interest was concentrated on the final end of the elect, not on the transitory satisfaction of the reprobate. The eternal welfare of the elect depended upon God and not upon themselves. To be happy, they needed to be conformed to the will of God, and whatever they might achieve through His will could only produce the confession: *we are unprofitable servants.*

Given this understanding of the nature of free will, it is hard to see how Augustinian theology can claim to provide for any satisfactory notion of responsibility on the part of the individual. Yet it does, and had so to provide, if it were to maintain the justice of God, as well as His mercy. Augustine did this by incorporating the whole human race into the person of Adam when he sinned in Paradise, so that all humanity sinned in him, and shared his responsibility. The intellectual difficulty which Augustine's theory of the seminal identity of the human race with Adam, and the justice of regarding humanity as sharing any moral responsibility for its progenitor's fall, is so enormous that it may seem amazing that the Augustinian doctrine of Original Sin so long dominated Western theology. Read with an appropriate disposition, it could be regarded as being constructed on a Pauline foundation, and the rôle which it assigned to concupiscence in the transmission of Original Sin could satisfy that spirit of encratitism which early entered Christianity; but denial of any possibility of salvation to anyone who died unbaptized, including infants, other than the martyrs—a doctrine repudiated by Calvin, though without naming Augustine[17]—is horrifying, and must have repelled many people down the ages who were afraid to oppose it openly.

It is generally accepted that the Greek Fathers, while admitting the fact of the Fall, preferred to understand its influence as a spiritual infection rather than as an inherited legal liability. This makes it possible for the individual to struggle against sin in a manner analogous to that envisaged by the Pelagians, and by the Semi-Pelagians, who drew upon the heritage of the Egyptian Desert. For Augustine, no such possibility is allowed: without God's immediate and direct aid, the individual cannot will, still less do, anything good; and if aid is given it is entirely gratuitous and in no way deserved—even Christ's human nature had not done anything to merit being united to the Word.[18] But Christ's human nature, uniquely, was without sin. Every other human being shared in the guilt of Adam and rightly deserved eternal condemnation.

Augustine's view of the consequences of Adam's sin stems from his understanding of the high state which Adam enjoyed in Paradise before the Fall, which is so enthusiastically described in *De Civitate Dei* XIV.26, and the catastrophic nature of his sin:

17. Calvin, *Institutio*, ed. Benoît, 4,15,20: "I answer that this teaching is madness. In telling us that He will be the God of our seed after us, God declares that He adopts our children and keeps them for his own before they are born." Calvin's position is based on 1 Corinthians 7:14. He is not concerned with the children of non-Christian parents.

18. *Ench.* 11,36: "Quid enim natura humana in homine Christo meruit, ut in unitatem personae unici filii dei singulariter esset assumpta? Quae bona voluntas, cuius boni propositi studium, quae bona opera praecesserunt, quibus mereretur iste homo una fieri persona cum deo?" *CCL* 46,69.

> God, the author of natures not of vices, made man upright. Man, wilfully depraved and justly condemned, gave birth to descendants equally depraved and condemned. We were all in that one person and we were all that one person, who fell into sin through the agency of the woman, the woman who had been made out of him before the sin.[19]

Augustine here develops the Pauline image of humanity being either *in Adam* or *in Christ,* though for him we were all in Adam, while only the elect are in Christ. Augustine seems to have taken an image literally, and so contrived to visit Adam's personal sin on his descendants. Furthermore, his belief that, martyrdom apart, there is no possibility of salvation for anyone who dies unbaptized, meant inevitably that the overwhelming majority of the human race is doomed to damnation,[20] and Augustine did not shrink from saying so, though he did urge that discretion should be exercised in proclaiming his doctrine from the pulpit.

Augustine's harshness might be attributed to the spirit of his age, which saw the beginning of the attack on the theology of Origen and his condemnation at Rome in 400, a condemnation to which Augustine subscribed.[21] However, even in his own day Julian of Eclanum was repelled by Augustine's views, and Augustine himself was disturbed by them, as appears from his letter to Jerome of 415:

> I ask you, where can the soul of an infant snatched away by death, have contracted the guilt which, unless the Grace of Christ come to the rescue by that sacrament of baptism which is administered even to infants, involves it in condemnation? . . . Where . . . is the justice of the condemnation of so many thousands of souls which, in the deaths of infant children, leave the world without the benefit of the Christian sacrament?[22]

About the same time that this letter to Jerome was written, or a little earlier, Augustine, writing to his friend Evodius, bishop of Uzalis, was

19. *Civ.* 13,14. *CCL* 48.395. Tr. Wand.

20. *Cor. et grat.*10,28: "Quod ergo pauci in comparatione pereuntium, in suo numero multi liberantur, gratia fit, gratis fit, gratiae sunt agendae quia fit, ne quis velut de suis meritis extollatur, sed omne os obstruatur (Rom. 3:19), ut qui gloriatur, in Domino glorietur." *PL* 44,933.

21. *Civ.* 21,17. *CCL* 48,783.

22. *Ep.* 166,3,6; 4,10. *CSEL* 44,554; 560–61.

to ask who would not rejoice if all the souls in Hell were to be set free, and especially those of poets, orators, and philosophers?[23] However brutal he may have been in defending what he considered to be the faith of the Church, and however bitterly sarcastic he may have been in his anti-pagan polemic, as witness the famous passage in Book V of *The City of God,* denouncing the thirst for glory of the great men of ancient Rome: *they have received their reward,*[24] Augustine did not, in his heart, rejoice over the damnation of the reprobate. He sought to balance the omnipotent justice of God with God's infinite mercy, and omnipotence triumphed. He was convinced that only the baptized are saved, and not all of them. Holding such views, which were probably widely shared in his own day, he was constrained to the predestinarian position which he was to maintain, not only at the end of his life against the Semi-Pelagians, but more than a decade earlier, in the hour of African triumph over Pelagius and Caelestius.

With such an outlook, it is not surprising that the condition of Adam, who embodied the human race, in Eden, should have exercised the mind of Augustine, for Adam in Eden was free, as his descendants have not been free since the Fall. As a created being he was conditioned by the will of God, his Creator; but he was left free to defy that will if he chose, even though the consequences would be disastrous. Augustine was to begin his consideration of Adam in the *De Libero Arbitrio,* commenced at Rome in 388 and completed in 395/6. The *De Libero Arbitrio* is an anti-Manichaean work which was concerned, by definition, to maintain the individual's freedom of choice in the face of Manichaean dualistic determinism. However, Augustine had to take into account the fact, of which he was aware from personal experience, that since the Fall the individual has no longer the freedom of choice which Adam was allowed in Eden. He therefore used Adam as the example of how man was originally created. Pelagius, at a later date, misunderstood this, and in the *De Natura*

23. *Ep.* 164,2,4: "si enim omnes omnino dixerimus tunc esse liberatos, qui illic inventi sunt, quis non gratuletur, si hoc possimus ostendere?" *CSEL* 44,524.

24. *Civ.* 5,15. *CCL* 47,149.

quoted three passages from the *De Libero Arbitrio* as supporting his own theological understanding of human nature as it is today, whereas Augustine spoke of it as it existed before the Fall, which Fall the Pelagians commonly denied.

When Augustine came to compose Books XII–XIV of *The City of God* in 418–20, he painted a picture of Adam before the Fall in the brightest colors: Adam surpassed all other living creatures on this earth in reason and understanding (XII, 24), a superiority indicated by his erect stature and demonstrated by his ability to name the animals. He enjoyed perfect health and a mind free from the disturbance of passion.[25] The only command laid upon him was a simple one of obedience—so long as he did not eat the forbidden apple, he could do as he liked, within the limitations of his created nature, and live for ever.[26] In short, Adam enjoyed a state of happiness unknown to his fallen descendants, and it is difficult—perhaps one should say, impossible—to understand how he was ever mad enough to disobey and end his idyllic existence.

In the third book of *De Libero Arbitrio,* written about 395, Augustine had in some degree discussed the question. In *The City of God,* Book XII (about 418), he described Adam as being created "as a kind of mean between angels and beasts."

> . . . so that if he submitted to his Creator, as to his true sovereign Lord, and observed his instructions with dutiful obedience, he should pass over into the fellowship of the angels, attaining an immortality of endless felicity without any intervening death; but if he used his free will in arrogance and disobedience, and thus offended God, his Lord, he should live like the beasts, under sentence of death; should be the slave of his desires; and destined after death for eternal punishment.[27]

In the *De Libero Arbitrio* Augustine had considered the problem more philosophically: sin is the consequence of the Fall, whether we sin by ignorance or feebleness, and what we call sin takes its origin from the primal sin, committed by free will. A wise man will not sin, a fool sins

25. Ibid., 14,26. *CCL* 48,449.
26. Ibid., 14,15. *CCL* 48,436–7.
27. Ibid.,12,22. *CCL* 47,380.

inevitably. Adam was created in an intermediate condition, being neither wise nor foolish, but capable of either folly or wisdom. Folly is not any kind of ignorance of things to be sought or avoided, but ignorance which is due to man's own fault *(vitiosa ignorantia)*. A wise man would not sin; but an intermediate being endowed with free will could receive a commandment which he could observe, and if he failed to do so, would be guilty of rebellion against his Creator.

It is not to be wondered at that man, through ignorance, has not the freedom of will to choose to do what he ought; or that he cannot see what he ought to do or fulfil it when he will, in face of carnal custom which, in a sense, has grown as strong, almost, as nature because of the power of mortal succession. It is the most just penalty of sin that man should lose what he was unwilling to make good use of, when he could have done so without difficulty if he had wished.[28]

Thus, Augustine's understanding of the nature of the Fall was the same in 394/5, long before the Pelagian Controversy had broken out, as it was in 418.

But more than that. By 394/5 Augustine was fully persuaded that fallen human nature had been radically vitiated by Adam's sin.

All that a man does wrongfully in ignorance, and all things that he cannot do rightly though he wishes to do so, are called sins, because they have their origin in the first sin of the will when it was free.[29]

However, Augustine was still, at that time, prepared to allow some initiative to righteousness on the part of Adam's descendants:

That Adam should have begotten children better than himself was not equitable; but if any of Adam's race should be willing to turn to God, and so overcome the punishment which had been merited by the original turning from God, it was fitting not only that he should not be hindered but that he should also receive divine aid. In this way the Creator showed how easily man might have retained, if he had so willed, the nature with which he was created, because his offspring had power to transcend that in which he was born.[30]

28. *Lib. arb.* 3,18,52. *CCL* 29,305–306. Tr. Burleigh.
29. Ibid. 3,19,54. *CCL* 29,306. Tr. Burleigh.
30. Ibid. 3,19,55. *CCL* 29,307. Tr. Burleigh.

In this passage there remains a hint of initiative in fallen humanity, which Augustine was to abandon, in theory, a year or two later, when writing to Simplicianus of Milan. There is, however, a difference between theological theory and pastoral practice. Augustine was well aware of the need to preserve the morale of his congregation, as when he urged that his predestinarian doctrine should be expounded discreetly, so that individuals are not continually reminded of the absolute character of the divine decree, by which some are chosen and others rejected, to the dismay of simple and sensitive minds.[31] Furthermore, in dealing with individuals, Augustine always acted as if they had the power to make their own decisions. We find this, for example, in the model which he provides in *De Catechezandis Rudibus* for addressing a potential convert, who is congratulated on having given thought of true and certain security in the great and perilous tempests of this present life[32] and for wishing to be made a Christian for the sake of the eternal happiness and perpetual rest which is promised in the future to the saints.[33] The *De Catechizandis Rudibus* was written about 400. Some years later, probably early in 413, Augustine wrote the *De Fide et Operibus (On Faith and Works)*. In this book (14, 21) he mentions that he had, in the *De Spiritu et Littera* of 412, treated of St. Paul's declaration that we are justified by faith, and not by observance of the Law (Rom. 3:28; Gal. 2:16) as meaning, not that faith alone is necessary for justification, but *faith working by love* (Gal. 5:6).[34] In *De Fide et Operibus* Augustine develops this theme. He was concerned, he says, with the views of certain persons who held that it was possible to achieve salvation by faith alone, without good works.[35] Accordingly, they maintained, any candidate for baptism should be admitted, however evil his way of life and even if he had no intention of changing it. This feeling stemmed partly from sympathy for persons denied baptism because of their way of life or whose baptism was delayed for the same mor-

31. *Dono pers.* 22,57–61. *PL* 45,1028–30.
32. *Cat. rud.* 16,24,2. *CCL* 46,148–9.
33. Ibid., 17,27,4. *CCL* 46,152.
34. *Fid. et op.* 14,21. *CSEL* 41,62.
35. Ibid., 1,1. *CSEL* 41,35–36; cf. *retr.* 2,38[64]. *CCL* 57,121.

al reason; but also from a belief in an automatic salvation conferred by the sacraments, without regard to any intention of amendment of life on the part of the recipient,[36] which reduced the sacraments to magical charms. Augustine could not deny the presence of bad Christians in the Church. It was for him a basic assumption, from which he drew his theology of the Two Cities, that the good and the bad are currently united in the Church Militant and must be tolerated until the final separation,[37] but that does not mean that we should accept candidates for baptism without a promise of amendment of life before the reception of the sacrament.[38] Augustine expresses the issue with some forcefulness:

> Let us suppose that a man comes and asks to be baptized, but says that he will not give up sacrificing to idols unless, perhaps, at some future time, he so wills. This man is not only a worshipper of idols but also a priest of some abominable cult. Nevertheless, he asks to be baptized immediately, and to become the Temple of the living God. I ask our opponents if they think that such a person should be admitted even as a catechumen? Most assuredly they will say that he should not be admitted, and I do not at all doubt that they are sincere.[39]

Let it be clear what Augustine is here saying: he demands a positive moral action from an individual before he has received the grace of baptism. It was, of course, the practice of the Church with regard to admission to the catechumenate and Augustine accepted it—he could not, by his own principles, do otherwise. Equally, by his own principles, he would regard the candidate's decision to be possible only by the grace of God; but the fact remains that he was assuming the possibility of willing a good action by one who was unregenerate. Augustine referred to the *De Fide et Operibus* in his *Enchiridion,* or "Handbook of Christian Doctrine," written about 421, emphasizing that the faith which saves is *faith*

36. *Civ.* 21,25. *CCL* 48,795.

37. *Cat. rud.* 19,31,1: "Neque hoc nos movere debet, quia multi diabolo consentiant, et pauci deum sequuntur; quia et frumentum in comparatione palearum valde pauciorem habet numerum. Sed sicut agricola novit quid faciat de ingenti acervo paleae, sic nihil est deo multitudo peccatorum, qui novit quid de illis agat, ut administratio regni eius ex nulla parte turbetur." *CCL* 46,155; cf. *fid. et op.*, 5,7. *CSEL* 41,42–3.

38. *Fid. et op.*, 6,8. *CSEL* 41,43–4.

39. Ibid., 12,18. *CSEL* 41,57–8.

working through love (Gal. 5:6); "but if faith works evil rather than good, without doubt, as the apostle James says, it is *dead in itself*" (Jas. 2:17).[40] Augustine returned to this theme in Book XXI of *The City of God:*

> Nor should those who remain as if in communion with the Catholic Church to the end of their lives feel any confidence when considering the text: *He who perseveres to the end will be saved* (Matt. 10:22), if they abandon the righteousness of life which Christ is to them (cf. Rom. 10:3) by the wickedness of their life, by fornication, by perpetrating in their bodies those impurities which the Apostle was unwilling to name (1 Cor. 5:1), or by abandoning themselves to shameful self-indulgence, or doing any of the things of which the Apostle says: those who do such things will not inherit the kingdom of God (Gal. 5:21).[41]

Such language clearly implies that the individual is responsible for his actions and may fairly be compared with Pelagius's assertion: "In the day of judgment no mercy will be shown to sinners but they will be burned in eternal fires."[42] The problem is to reconcile Augustine's language in his anti-Pelagian writings with his assumption of free choice in human life. Pierre-Marie Hombert, in his massive and massively learned book *Gloria Gratiae,* has argued that Augustine's predestinarian teaching is inspired by the intention of a mystic and pastor to warn his hearers against the sin of pride, rather than to express satisfaction at the fate of the damned.[43] This may be the case—Augustine was certainly ready, on occasion, "to lose himself in a mystery and to pursue his reason to an *O altitudo*"—but the ruthlessness of his reasoning, even if based, as many would hold, on faulty premises, makes it difficult to believe that he did not take his final system literally.

40. *Ench.* 18,67. *CCL* 46,85–6.
41. *Civ.* 21,25,4. *CCL* 48,795.
42. *Gest. Pel.* 3,9. *CSEL* 42,60; Jerome, *Dialogus* 1,28. *PL* 23,544.
43. Hombert, *Gloria Gratiae,* pp. 441ff., 573ff.

CHAPTER 5

AUGUSTINE'S FINAL THEOLOGY OF FREEDOM

AT THE END OF HIS LIFE, when his relentless insistence on divine predestination had led to the accusation that he had reduced human freedom to a cipher, Augustine continued to maintain freedom of choice by the elect, despite the vital necessity of grace to enable them to exercise that freedom, and provided an argument to explain it. In about 425 a copy of his Letter 194, written in 418/9 at the crisis of the Pelagian dispute to the presbyter Sixtus, a future bishop of Rome,[1] arrived at the monastery of Hadrumetum in Byzacena, the modern Tunisia. In this letter Augustine had presented his doctrine of predestination in terms which seemed to some members of the community to make human beings mere instruments in the hand of God. In a letter of explanation to the monks of Hadrumetum, Augustine declared that the letter to Sixtus had been intended to refute the notion that grace was given as a reward for merit—a belief which would lead to the sin of pride—and urged those who could not understand the relation of divine grace and freedom of choice to accept both as revealed truths of Scripture, and to pray that they should be given understanding.[2] Augustine maintained, with many scriptural quotations, that free choice existed in the fallen human will, but could only be exercised for good after the reception of the gift of grace. One of the letters, discovered and first published by Johannes

1. *Ep.* 194. *CSEL* 57,176–214.
2. *Ep.* 214,7. *CSEL* 57,386–7.

Divjak in 1981, provides an illustration of how Augustine resolved the question, at least to his own satisfaction.

The letter in question (Letter 2*), written between 426 and 428, was addressed to a certain Firmus, a leisured intellectual, interested in theological discussion but still unbaptized and anxious to defer baptism as long as possible, in order that he might continue to enjoy adulterous sexual liaisons, such as were taken for granted by many nominally Christian men, but which would have to be renounced after receiving the sacrament. From Augustine's point of view the matter was by no means an academic one: if Firmus died unbaptized he would infallibly be damned. At the same time, Augustine may have felt some sympathy with Firmus, remembering his own problems at Milan on the eve of his conversion in 386. Logically, Augustine might obviously have refrained from urging Firmus to take action and left him to the mercy of God. In his famous verdict on the treatise *Ad Simplicianum* (397), recorded in the *Retractations,* he had succinctly summed up his conclusions: "In the solution of this question I labored in defense of the free choice of the human will, but the grace of God conquered, and I was finally able to understand, with perfect clarity, the meaning of the Apostle: *For who singles you out? And what do you have that you did not receive? And if you received it, why do you boast as if it were not a gift?*" (1 Cor. 4:7).[3] This text was to be decisive for Augustine from 397 to the end of his life. For him, in the final analysis, God had to be supreme and man could hold no claim whatever to be independent of his Maker. However, Scripture and pastoral experience alike witnessed to an apparent element of self-determination subsisting in the human mind. Certainly God's will cannot ultimately be frustrated, and those who think that they are thwarting Him are, in fact, fulfilling His final purposes,[4] but our belief that when we will we do in fact will is not to be regarded as mere fantasy: there is genuine volition. Unhap-

3. *Retr.* II,1 [27/28]. *CCL* 57,89–90.

4. *Civ.* 22,2. *CCL* 48,807–8; cf. 5,9,4: "qua propter et voluntates nostrae tantum valent, quantum deus eas voluit atque praescivit." *CCL* 47,140.

pily, because of the Fall, free will avails only for sin, unless it is assisted by divine grace. In order, then, to observe God's commandments, fallen human will must be prepared by God—*praeparatur voluntas a Domino* (Prov. 8:35 LXX).[5] Only then can we will what is good, since unless it is assisted by divine grace, free will avails only for sin.[6] *The good that I would I do not; but the evil that I would not, that I do* (Rom. 7:19). Accordingly, in urging Firmus to take the decision which would make him potentially one of the elect—for baptism, if not followed by a deliberately observed Christian life, does not automatically ensure salvation, as some people in Augustine's day believed[7]—Augustine sought to assure him that he both could, and should, make a decision, because God would have already given him the power to decide.

> Do not wait upon the moment when God may will this, as if you would offend Him if you were to will it before He did, because it is only when He is helping and cooperating that you can make the act of the will.[8]

To understand what Augustine is saying here, it must be remembered that, for him, human power to do good depends utterly and immediately on God: when God crowns human merits, He crowns His own works.[9] Since because of the Fall, free choice now avails only for sin,[10] Divine grace must restore the freedom which Adam enjoyed in Paradise. To do any good work, the individual must receive the gift of grace, after which he may, of his own volition, make his decision. So Augustine tells Firmus:

5. *Grat. et lib. arb.* 16,32. *PL* 42,900.

6. *Nat. et grat.* 3,3–5,5; 50,58; 55,65. *CSEL* 60,235–6; 275–6; 281–2.

7. *Civ.* 21,25,4. *CCL* 48,794–6.

8. *Ep.* 2*,7,5: "nec expectes quando velit, quasi offensurus eum si ante tu velis, cum ipso adiuvante et operante velis, quandocumque volueris." *CSEL* 88,14.

9. *Grat. et lib. arb.* 6,15. *PL* 44,890; *ep.* 194,5,19. *CSEL* 57,190.

10. *C. duas epp. Pel.* 1,2,5; 3,8,24: "et liberum arbitrium captivatum nonnisi ad peccatum valet; ad iustitiam vero, nisi divinitatus liberatum adiutumque, non valet." *CSEL* 60,425–6; 516; *cor. et grat.* 1,2: "liberum itaque arbitrium et ad malum et ad bonum faciendum confitendum est nos habere: sed in malo faciendo liber est quisque iustitiae servus peccati: in bono autem liber esse nullus potest, nisi fuerit liberatus ab eo qui dixit; *Si vos Filius liberaverit, tunc vere liberi eritis* (Ioh. 8:36)." *PL* 44,917.

> It is assuredly God's mercy that prompts you to make the act of your will; but when you make that act, it will certainly be you yourself doing so. For if we ourselves do not make any act of the will whenever we do in fact will something, then He does not confer on us anything at all when He enables us to use our wills.[11]

These words epitomize Augustine's idea of divine initiative and its relation to human freedom at the end of his life, when applied to his pastoral responsibility as a Christian minister. God is absolute: nothing can be done without His initiative, and for this reason He needs to give the power to act righteously. On the other hand, when he *has* received the power, an individual is free to exercise it or not. Man cannot act without God's help; but after being given that help, he is a free agent.

This being said, two devastating qualifications are to be noted. God does not will to give grace to everyone. This is particularly clear in the case of baptism: two children are born; both pertaining to the mass of sin, brought about by the Fall. One is brought to baptism by its mother, the other is suffocated by its mother in her sleep.[12] The one is potentially saved, the other is condemned. Why should this be, when neither has added any personal sins to that inherited from Adam? The reason for this distinction will be made clear at the General Resurrection; now it can only be a mystery.[13] This, however, leads to the second qualification: God does not have an absolute intention to save every human being, and no individual human being, whatever his hopes and desire for God may be, can do anything about this; no Christian, as long as he lives, can know whether he is predestinated to salvation.[14] Yet conversely, on the human side, all human beings, while they are still in the body, must be regarded pastorally as potentially predestined to grace, and so Augus-

11. *Ep.* 2*,7,6: "praevenit quidem te misericordia eius, ut velis, sed cum voles tu utique voles. nam si nos non volumus, quando volumus, non ergo nobis ille confert aliquid, cum efficit ut velimus." *CSEL* 88,14.

12. *Serm.* 26,13. *CCL* 41,357.

13. *Ench.* 24,95. *CCL* 46,99.

14. *Cor. et grat.* 13,40. *PL* 44, 940–41.

tine could urge Firmus to make the decision to receive baptism, without which salvation is impossible.[15]

It is here that the so-called Semi-Pelagian theologians of Marseilles reacted against Augustine. For them man, even though fallen, retained an element of decision, as a result of the natural good which God had implanted in him at his creation, and might therefore turn to God by his own initiative, even though that initiative ultimately comes from God.[16] There is a similar implication in Pelagius's analysis of the factors involved in a moral action: the power to perform it; the will to perform it; and the performance itself.[17] The first of these depends upon God; the other two on man. Hence, reasoned Pelagius, in good actions

> we praise both human beings and God who gave them the ability for this will and action and who always assists this ability by the help of His grace. That one element, then, can exist, even if these other two do not. But these other two cannot exist without the former. I am free, therefore, to have neither my will nor my action good, but I cannot fail to have the ability to do good. It is present in me, even if I do not want it.[18]

Augustine (perhaps deliberately?) misunderstood Pelagius's assertion that the ability of the individual to do good is continually present in the human will as representing a potentiality to be activated on occasion by the individual in making a decision, and he chose to interpret this as a deliberate diminution in the divine contribution to human good actions.

> We should certainly realize that [Pelagius] does not believe that either our will or our action is aided by God's help, but only by the endowment of the ability for willing and for acting. For of these three he claims that we only have the

15. *Ep.* 2*,6: "Propter eos tamen qui differendum putant quod bonum esse non negant, illa est divinarum scripturarum terribiliter intonata sententia: *Ne tardes converti ad dominum neque differas de die in diem! Subito enim veniet ira eius et in tempore vindictae disperdet te* (Eccl. 5:8–9)." *CSEL* 88,13.

16. Cassian, *Collatio* 13, esp. 13–14. *CSEL* 13,382–8. See Columba Stewart, *Cassian the Monk* (New York/London, 1998), 79–81.

17. *Grat. Christ. et pecc. orig.* 1,4,5. *CSEL* 42,127–8.

18. Ibid. Augustine, *Answer to the Pelagians (The Works of St. Augustine: A Translation for the 21st Century)*, introduction, translation, and notes by Raymond J. Teske, I, 23–25 (New York: New City Press, 1997–99).

ability from God. He implies that the element which God placed in our nature is weak, but that the other two, which Pelagius attributes to us, are so strong and powerful and self-sufficient that they do not need His help.[19]

What Augustine means by this interpretation in 418 is made clear in the light of his letter to Firmus in 426–28, where he tells his correspondent that "it is assuredly God's mercy which prompts you to make this act of your will."[20] For Augustine, every single good act requires an initial impulse from God to inspire the recipient to will. For Pelagius, the inspiration is already available and when the individual makes the act of will, it will be a genuine act of will for which he will be responsible.

One might say that for Pelagius, the power to do good resembles a bank account provided by God, upon which a man has freedom to draw when he chooses. If he draws, there is praise for him for doing so. If he fails to draw, he must bear the responsibility. For Augustine, there is no bank account: God bestows on man the power to act as He pleases. Accordingly, when He crowns our actions it is His own merits that He crowns and the individual earns no praise for his works. If he fails to respond, he suffers for his inherited guilt from Adam.

It may be asked why Augustine interpreted Pelagius as he did, in asserting that human volition and action are so strong that they do not need immediate prevenient help, an interpretation not justified by the text of 2 Timothy 4:6–8. One factor would be his mood in 418. In his first encounter with Pelagius's thought in 412 he had found Pelagius recounting other people's arguments against Original Sin without personally endorsing or denouncing them. In 416, after Pelagius's acquittal at the council of Diospolis, which initially seemed to suggest that the Greek churches had endorsed Pelagian theology, Augustine became completely hostile and was prepared to make the worst possible interpretation of Pelagian theology. In 418, after his condemnation by emperor and pope alike, Pelagius declared that divine grace was necessary, not only at every hour and at every moment, but also for every separate

19. Ibid., 1,5,6. *CSEL* 42,129. Tr. Teske, 1/23, p. 405.
20. *Ep.* 2*,7,6. *CSEL* 88,14.

human action[21]—essentially the inspiration of Augustine's own thinking; but Augustine was by now persuaded that Pelagius's understanding of grace was still in terms of law and teaching, and not in cooperation and the gift of love.[22] Robert Evans was persuaded that in this estimation Augustine was right in respect of Pelagius's surviving writings,[23] but this was not necessarily still the case in 418. However, Augustine was not prepared to show mercy.

The division between the two theologies, Pelagian and Augustinian, turns essentially upon their respective understanding of the nature of the Fall and the transmission of Original Sin. Whether Pelagius himself ever explicitly rejected the notion of Original Sin, as did his predecessor and possible teacher, Rufinus the Syrian, cannot be established. Pelagius was always concerned to avoid trouble, not to cause it—it was his misfortune that he had controversy thrust upon him against his desire; but whether he accepted the notion of Original Sin or not, he never denied that the power to do right was entirely of God. The difference between him and Augustine concerned the power to act righteously in human beings *at the present day.* Augustine held that the Fall had so weakened the human will that it required a separate impulse of divine grace for every righteous action. Pelagius asserted that the ability to will could be exercised by the individual at any time through the indwelling grace of God. In this respect he anticipated the Massilian theologians. For John Cassian, their most distinguished representative, God works in all human beings but grace is dispensed to humanity in various ways, according to individual personality. Sometimes the beginning of good works occurs as a consequence of the good implanted in human beings at their creation; at other times God's grace anticipates the individual will.[24] It

21. *Grat. Christ. et pecc. orig.* 1,2,2. *CSEL* 42,125. Tr. Teske, 1/23, p. 403.

22. Ibid., 1,3,3. *CSEL* 42,127. Tr. Teske, 1/23, p. 404.

23. R. F. Evans, *Pelagius: Inquiries and Reappraisals* (New York, 1968), 111: "Pelagius has no doctrine of grace other than this. It would be unfaithful to the man himself to attempt to save his 'orthodoxy' by reading in some doctrine of infused grace which is not there."

24. John Cassian, *Conlationes* 13,11; 14 and 15. Cf. 13,17,1. *CSEL* 13,375–8, 384–90, 392–4.

may be that Pelagius underestimated the influence of habit upon human power of decision, as did his defender, Julian of Eclanum: "Freedom of choice is as full after sins as it was before";[25] but he did not deny that power of decision comes from God.

The crucial determinant, then, is the state of humanity as it now is after Adam's expulsion from Eden. For Augustine, the Fall had so weakened man that he could only say: "Give what you command and command what You will"—a petition which outraged Pelagius,[26] for whom it represented an excuse made by those who wished to avoid responsibility for their decisions. Pelagius's attitude was psychologically relatively simple, the assumption upon which society rests, and to which, for practical purposes, Augustine himself subscribed in pastoral and secular matters; but Augustine's concerns went deeper, and touched the mystery of human nature. He was, however, conditioned by his fundamental assumption of the legacy of the Fall upon Adam's descendants. By complicated reasoning he involved Adam's children in an inherited guilt[27] and, in addition, he painted the gloomiest possible picture of the moral nature of fallen man, and man's inability to do anything but evil without God's immediate aid, in spite of his insistence on the goodness of God's creation and the non-material character of evil. It was not without reason that Julian of Eclanum declared that Augustine still remained influenced in his thinking by Manichaeism:[28] "We [anti-Augustinians] say that the sin of a human being does not change the state of nature, but the quality of the merit; that is, we say that there is in sinners the same nature of free choice by which they can stop sinning as was present in them that they could turn away from righteousness."[29] Augustine treated the present

25. Julian, *op. imp.* 1,91; 95. *CSEL* 85/1,104; 110. Tr. Teske, 1/25,115; 118.

26. *Conf.* 10,29,40. *CSEL* 33,256; *dono pers.* 20,53. *PL* 45,1026; cf. *sp. et litt.* 13,22. *CSEL* 60, 175–6.

27. See Bonner, *Augustine of Hippo*, 3rd ed., 370ff.

28. Julian, *op. imp.* 1,98: "ad Iovinianum consortium confugisti, sed Manichaei lupanar necdum reliquisti." *CSEL* 85/1,115.

29. *Op. imp.* 1,96: "[Iulianus]: Nos dicimus peccato hominis non naturae statum mutari, sed meriti qualitatem, id est et in peccante hanc esse liberi arbitrii naturam, per quam potest a peccato desinere, quae fuit ideo, ut posset a iustitia deviare." *CSEL* 85/1, 111. Tr. Teske 1/25, p. 119.

human "state of nature" in a physical sense, as essentially the loss of immortality consequent upon the Fall. Julian was concerned with the human mind and will independent of the body. He was certainly simplistic in his understanding of the working of the human will; but he recognized the enduring goodness of God's creation even in sinners, and the appeal of God even for those in a state of sin. Augustine's view of Original Sin is certainly grimmer than that of the majority of the Fathers; but it is often difficult for an admirer of Augustine—his detractors find no difficulty—to comprehend the sheer grimness of his theology.

Between Augustine and Julian a great and unbridgeable gulf had been fixed. Julian and his fellow-Pelagians lost the public battle and suffered a centuries-long condemnation, which only began to be revalued in the nineteenth century.[30] It is not necessary, in attempting to do the Pelagians justice, to present them as major theologians; but they opposed a note of reason to the dogmatism congenial to African spirituality, of which Augustine was the spokesman, which is to their credit. They are open to the criticism that their approach to Christian conduct could lead to a self-sufficiency which in turn could lead to pride—a danger which Augustine already saw in his treatise *De Gratia Novi Testamenti* (Ep. 140) of 412—and which, according to P.-M. Hombert, was the ultimate inspiration of his anti-Pelagian polemic.[31]

Pelagianism was not, as Augustine seems to have thought, either a mass movement or a coordinated theological school. Emphases differed. There were those who, like Rufinus the Syrian and Caelestius, were concerned to refute belief in the transmission of Original Sin. Others, like Pelagius, were more concerned to exhort to Christian living and to attempt a reasoned argument for the ability to do so. Julian of Eclanum, of whose great literary output more has survived than that of any other

30. Brooke Foss Westcott, for example, in an article in *The Contemporary Review* of 1878, thought that turning to Greek theology would lighten the Church from "the heavy burden of materialistic conceptions" imposed on it by Latin theology. See L. E. Eliott-Binns, *English Thought 1865–90: The Theological Aspect* (London, 1956), 222. On the other hand, Harnack, a liberal theologian, was bitterly hostile to Pelagius.

31. Hombert, *Gloria Gratiae*, pp. 160–71; 184–97; 255–84.

Pelagian, covered the whole range of the topics involved in the dispute with Augustine, but was particularly concerned to emphasize the righteousness of God, the free choice of man, and the innocence of human sexuality. God is just;[32] a just God does not consign newborn children, incapable of willing good or evil, to hellfire.[33] For Julian, sin is nothing else than the evil will of one who is free to abstain from evil.[34] The text *By one man sin entered into the world* (Rom. 5:12) refers to Adam alone, and we sin by imitating him, not through sharing in his sin.[35] The abundance of human sin demanded the abundant mercy of a generous God.[36] God did not lay demands on men that they were incapable of fulfilling.[37] The Law (Deut. 24:16) prescribes that the sins of the parents are not to be visited on the children; thus Original Sin is a Manichaean doctrine.[38] The form of baptism, by which we are sanctified, is the same for all ages; it says nothing of corrupt generation, or diabolical flesh, or of Adam, and gives no support to a doctrine of the transmission of sin.[39]

Julian argued at great length, and Augustine replied at greater, but the lines of battle were clearly drawn. The Pelagian case was that responsibility for sin could not be inherited: God would not visit the sins of the fathers upon the children. Augustine replied that God Himself punishes children for the sins of parents (Ex. 20:5), but tells human beings not to do so.[40] To what extent do the Pelagian protests damage Augustine's case for later generations of Christian thinkers?

The strongest Pelagian argument is that a just God will not hold individuals guilty of sins which they were powerless to avoid. This flatly dismisses the concept of the penal nature of Original Sin, to which Augustine was committed, defending it with the argument that what God does Himself He may forbid as unjust to His human creatures. Such a double

32. *Op. imp.* 1,28: "Ita enim omnibus generaliter edocente natura incalcatum est deum iustum esse, ut manifestum sit deum non esse, quem consteterit iustum non esse. Potest igitur et homo iustus esse; deus vero esse nisi iustus non potest." *CSEL* 85/1, 23.

33. Ibid., 1,48,2–3. *CSEL* 85/1,36–37.

34. Ibid., 2,17. *CSEL* 85/1,174.

35. Ibid., 2,56,1. *CSEL* 85/1,203.

36. Ibid., 2,222,1. *CSEL* 85/1,335.

37. Ibid., 3,4. *CSEL* 85/1,353.

38. Ibid., 3,36. *CSEL* 85/1,376.

39. Ibid., 1,53,2; 3,59. *CSEL* 85/1,48; 399.

40. Ibid., 3,36. *CSEL* 85/1 376.

standard of divine justice would be generally as unacceptable today as it was to Julian of Eclanum, and invites the retort of John Stuart Mill: "I will call no being good who is not what I mean when I apply that epithet to my fellow creatures." Again, Augustine's easy acceptance of the view that the great majority of the human race, including unbaptized infants, will be damned, would be rejected by many today who would not call themselves Pelagians, but who would nevertheless be inclined to echo Caelestius: "I have told you that as regards the transmission of sin I have heard various people within the Catholic Church deny it and others assert it. It therefore follows that it is a matter of opinion, not of heresy. I have always said that infants need baptism and ought to be baptized."[41] It is possible to understand Original Sin as an hereditary infection, without believing that it carries with it inherited guilt.

In the mystery of the relation between God's omnipotence and human freedom and responsibility, the Pelagians emphasized freedom in order to establish responsibility. Pelagius was accused of having said that on the day of judgment no mercy would be shown to sinners but they would be burned in eternal fires,[42] which he defended by quoting Matthew 25:46: *Sinners will go away into eternal punishment, but the righteous into eternal life,* and adding that anyone who believed differently was an Origenist.[43] Julian of Eclanum emphasized that it is the freedom to abstain which makes an action sinful, declaring that

> as justice itself judges, which does not impute a sin unless one is free to hold back, the people who sinned without the law will be judged without the law, and those who sinned under the law will be judged under the law.[44]

Pelagius had years before written to the virgin Demetrias, assuring her that God did not impose impossible commands on men.[45] At the Synod of Diospolis he was wrongly accused of having written: "Evil does not even enter one's thoughts," which he explained as meaning that a

41. *Grat. Christ. et pecc. orig.,* 2,3,3–4,4. *CSEL* 42,168–69.

42. *Gest. Pel.* 3,9. *CSEL* 42,60.

43. Ibid., 10. *CSEL* 42,60–61.

44. *Op. imp.* 2,187. *CSEL* 85/1, 304.

45. Pelagius, *Ad Demetriaden* 2. *PL* 30,17; 33,1100.

Christian ought to strive not to think evil.[46] The reliability of Pelagius's defense has been questioned; but his position is clear: man has the power to avoid sin if he chooses to do so. That power, however, comes from God, and is bestowed upon His creation, which remains dependent upon Him. Augustine countered this by saying that an emancipated son was no longer a member of his father's household;[47] though in popular estimation emancipation did not make him any less a son, who had duties to a father, and the freedman, a former slave, was no less closely bound by moral obligations. "A Roman freed slave is a half- or a quarter-citizen according to the precise formality of his manumission."[48] Man's power of decision comes from God, and the degree to which he enjoys it is determined by God the Creator, and not by man the creature, whether or not we accept the doctrine of Original Sin.

For Augustine, the case was utterly different. He not only believed in the doctrine of the Fall, but saw it as having had a decisive effect upon the human race, leaving mankind helpless without the immediate aid of God for any good act, even though we retain free will to do evil. It was this imputation of helplessness which enabled Julian of Eclanum to accuse Augustine of having remained a Manichee at heart, under the robe of a Catholic bishop, and it is a feature of Augustine's later thought, on occasion seeming to justify Thomas Allin's assertion that "his theology is *really a pathology;* he is *par excellence* a penologist . . . Instead of a theology, he gives us an elaborate criminology."[49] Allin considered that there are two theologies in Augustine: an earlier "catholic" doctrine, and a later one, produced by the maturer workings of his mind.[50] It is likely that this later theology was produced by the intellectual conversion which he experienced when writing to Simplicianus in 396, which persuaded Au-

46. *Gest. Pel.* 4,12. *CSEL* 42,63. On this see C. C. Burnett, "Dysfunction at Diospolis: A Comparative Study of Augustine's *De Gestis Pelagii* and Jerome's *Dialogus adversus Pelagianos,*" *Augustinian Studies* 34 (2003): 166–67.

47. *Op. imp.* 1,78. *CSEL* 85/1,93.

48. A. N. Sherwin White, *Roman Society and Roman Law in the New Testament* (Oxford, 1963), 158.

49. Allin, *The Augustinian Revolution in Theology* (London, 1911), 129,175–6.

50. Ibid., pp. 107ff.

gustine that the grace of God was stronger than freedom of choice; but from then onwards the cast of his mind was anti-Pelagian, even before he ever read a work of Pelagius, and this cast of thought was reinforced by his high estimation of the virtue of humility. To him the suggestion that a man could take the initiative in doing good smacked of pride, and he disparaged Pelagius's admission that the power to do good was of God and not of man.

Even if we allow for this, Augustine's picture of the state of fallen man is curious, given his conviction that all God's creation is good. The glowing picture of Adam's state in Paradise, which Augustine paints in Book XIV of *The City of God*,[51] is replaced by bodily mortality and the threat of eternal damnation, so that Adam's descendants belong to the condemned mass,[52] and Augustine complacently discusses the nature of eternal punishment,[53] including the character of hellfire, which is able to torment spiritual beings like the demons, who lack material bodies.[54] In the *Enchiridion ad Laurentium* he spares his reader any discussion of the nature of the resurrected bodies of the damned: "there is no need to expend effort in inquiring whether they will rise with the defects and deformities of their bodies and whatever defective and deformed limbs they had formerly. Nor should we weary ourselves by considering their appearance or beauty, since their damnation will be certain and unending."[55] There is a callousness in Augustine's attitude to the reprobate which revolted an agnostic liberal like J. B. Bury[56] and which has to be set beside, and contrasted with, the emphasis he lays on love as the defining characteristic of God the Creator and His Elect. In his lack of concern with the fate of those excluded from the mercy of God, Augustine was

51. *Civ.* 14,26. *CCL* 48,449.
52. *Nat. et grat.* 3,3–5,5. *CSEL* 60,235–6.
53. E.g. *civ.* 21,9. *CCL* 48,774–5.
54. *Civ.* 21,10. *CCL* 48,775–6.
55. *Ench.* 23,92. *CCL* 46,98–99.
56. Bury, *History of the Later Roman Empire*, vol. 1 (1923), 305–6: "There is at least one part [of the *dCD*] which may hold the attention of the reader, fascinated by the very horror, the Book [XXI] in which this arch-advocate of theological materialism and vindictive punishment expends all his ingenuity in proving that the fire of hell is literal fire and spares no effort to cut off the slenderest chance that the vast majority of his fellow-beings will not be tormented throughout eternity."

hardly unique in his age; and he takes care to refute the error, "promoted by tenderness of heart and human compassion," of those who suppose that the miseries of those condemned at the Last Judgment will be only temporal[57] or that the intercession of the saints will avail for those who commit grievous sins.[58] Even more repelling is his acceptance of the damnation of unbaptized babies, which caused Julian of Eclanum to say that Augustine worshipped a God who was a spiritual baby-batterer.[59]

Julian's observation is not simply polemical. It was a logical deduction on his part from the denial of any transmission of Original Sin. At Caelestius's trial at Carthage in 411, one of the allegations levelled against him was that he taught that mankind as a whole did not die through Adam's death nor rise through Christ's Resurrection.[60] The logic behind this was the assumption that Adam's sin injured only himself and not the human race, so that infants today are born in the state of Adam before he sinned. Furthermore, the Old Testament witnesses that before the coming of Christ, there had been sinless individuals.[61] Accordingly, such persons would have had no need for baptism *for the remission of sins,* though Caelestius did not dispute the desirability of infant baptism in his own age, now that it had been instituted by Christ.[62] For Augustine, this was wholly unacceptable. Only baptism could save from damnation; therefore for the unbaptized there could be no hope. Moreover, it is difficult to overemphasize Augustine's belief in the appalling consequences of Adam's sin transmitted to his descendants, which Rufinus the Syrian, Caelestius, and Julian denied. In the short work *Definitiones,* anonymous but attributed to Caelestius, the question is posed: is sin natural or an addition to nature? Caelestius argued:

57. *Civ.* 21,17. *CCL* 48,783; *ench.* 18,67. *CCL* 46,75.

58. *Civ.* 21,18. *CCL* 48,784.

59. *Op. imp.* 1,48,4: "deus . . . ipse sic iudicat, ipse est nascentium persecutor, ipse pro mala voluntate aeternis ignibus parvulos tradit, quos nec bonam nec malam voluntatem scit habere potuisse." *CSEL* 85/1,38.

60. *Grat. Christ. et pecc. orig.* 2,2,2. *CSEL* 42,167–8; Marius Mercator, *Commonitorium super nomen Coelestii* 1. *PL* 48,70A.

61. *Grat. Christ. et pecc. orig.* 2,4,3. *CSEL* 42,169.

62. Ibid., 2,4,4. *CSEL* 42,169.

If it is something natural, it is not a sin, but if it is an addition to nature, it can be removed [by baptism] as well. And what can be removed can be avoided, and a human being can be without what can be avoided, because it can be avoided.[63]

Augustine's reply was short and uncompromising:

My answer is that sin is not something natural. But we have become *by nature children of wrath* (Eph. 2:3), and for nature, and especially for injured nature, the choice of the will is of little use for avoiding sin, unless it is helped and healed by *the grace of God through Jesus Christ, our Lord* (Rom. 7:25).[64]

Despite the harshness of his attitude to the fate of the reprobate, Augustine's sense of the need for the grace of Christ, the God-man, marks him off from Pelagianism, in whatever form it presents itself. Sebastian Thier has noticed a contrast between Pelagius's ascetic ideal and that of Augustine: for Pelagius, the holiness of the Church derives from the holiness of her members; for Augustine it comes from the holiness of Christ, whose Body the Church is.[65] This belief does not, in itself, invalidate the Pelagian view, that the divine grace which makes a righteous action possible remains in each individual, and can be drawn upon by an act of will at any time; but it could provoke the self-satisfaction and pride which Augustine so feared as the particular temptation of those who aspired to be holy. *Without me, ye can do nothing.* Since Augustine was always concerned to inculcate the virtue of humility, it is easy to understand why he recoiled from Pelagian doctrine without giving it or its formulators a fair hearing. In itself there was nothing heretical in postulating that God had left some initiative in man and Augustine was constrained, by his own first principles, to admit that some trace of the divine image remains in fallen humanity.[66] The notion may be found in the anti-Pelagian Cassian. Augustine's rejection could only stem from his view of the catastrophic results of the Fall. From the exalted state of Adam in Paradise, described with such enthusiasm in *The City of God*

63. *Perf. iust. hom.* 2,3. *CSEL* 42,5. Tr. Teske.

64. Ibid.

65. Thier, *Die Kirche bei Pelagius* (Berlin/New York, 1999), 322.

66. *Sp. et litt.* 28,48. *CSEL* 60,202.

(XIV,25), Adam fell, like the angels before him,[67] through pride,[68] with terrible consequences for soul and body alike, and the guilt of his rebellion passed to his descendants. By a curious irony, Augustine held that Adam and Eve, by living righteously after the Fall, were saved by the blood of Christ,[69] while accepting that myriads of their descendants, who had committed no sin, were lost by the lack of baptism.

67. *Civ.* 11,33. *CCL* 48,352.
68. Ibid., 14,12–15. *CCL* 48,433–8.
69. *Pecc. mer. et rem.* 2,34,55. *CSEL* 60,125.

CHAPTER 6

DIVINE PREDESTINATION AND JESUS CHRIST

THE MORE THAT ONE CONSIDERS Augustine's theories of man's Fall and Redemption, the more difficult it becomes to understand how the various elements hold together, logically and theologically. Salvation is extended to only a tiny minority of the human race,[1] while the overwhelming majority is rejected. Augustine falls back—indeed is compelled to fall back—upon the hidden and inscrutable justice of God, witnessed by Scripture.[2] While Augustine on occasion anticipated later tendencies in scriptural criticism,[3] there were certain texts—for example, those which taught the necessity of baptism for salvation[4]—which he would not accept in any way other than literally. Universal salvation had been rejected in the Church in his own day, and Augustine, while he spoke of Origen with respect,[5] supported the rejection.[6] But to the text of Scripture should be added the cast of Augustine's mind; the conversion of 396 had had its effect. Man was wholly dependent upon God

1. *Cor. et grat.* 10,28. *PL* 44,933.

2. *Ench.* 24,95. *CSEL* 46,99; *grat. et lib. arb.* 23,45. *PL* 44,910.

3. See the *De Consensu Evangelistarum,* where Augustine recognizes that reported conversations need not be verbatim (2,12,29); acknowledges that individual authors may differ in their order of narration (2,21,51); and remarks upon the mistaken attribution of a quotation from Zechariah to Jeremiah in Matthew 27:9 (3,7,29). *CSEL* 43,129; 152;304–5.

4. *Pecc. mer. et rem.* 1,16,21; 18,23. *CSEL* 60,20–21; 22–23; cf. *c. duas epp. Pel.* 4,4,8. *CSEL* 60,528–9; *ep.* 166,7,21. *CSEL* 44,575–7; *ep.* 193,2,3. *CSEL* 57,168–70.

5. *Civ.* 11,23. *CCL* 48,341–3.

6. Ibid., 21,17: "sed illum et propter hoc, et propter alia nonulla . . . non immerito reprobavit ecclesia." *CCL* 48,783.

and, after the Fall, human initiative could only come from God immediately. It had been otherwise in Paradise,[7] it would be otherwise in heaven;[8] but at the present time, in the fallen world in which we live, a positive decision to act righteously required immediate divine inspiration. Human freedom was constricted by human weakness.

Yet this negative outlook had inevitably to be tempered by experience. Whatever the theory, a possible convert like Firmus, or any individual who came to the church at Hippo, had to be treated as a free agent, capable of making a decision.[9] Augustine cannot have forgotten his own decision in the garden at Milan,[10] but even more, he was aware of the desire for God, even in the fallen human soul. Recent studies have drawn attention to the attraction of God's beauty for the human soul, and to the instinct of desire in man which has made the sentence at the beginning of *The Confessions:* "Thou has made us for Thyself, and our heart knows no rest until it may repose in Thee,"[11] the favorite Augustinian quotation for so many readers.[12] Human beings were created by God, both to glorify Him and to enjoy Him, their Creator and the source of their well-being, who made them out of love and continues to love them in their rebellion and sin.

The problem in assessing the apparently contradictory theology of Augustine—and it is a major problem, in seeking to understand this man who has so influenced the thought of the Christian West and has attracted such differing evaluations—is the contrast between his optimism as a

7. Ibid., 14,10. *CCL* 48,430–31; cf. *lib.arb.* 3,1,1–7. *CSEL* 74,89–91.

8. *Civ.* 22,30,3: "Nec ideo liberum arbitrium non habebunt, quia peccata eos delectare non poterunt. Magis quippe erit liberum a dilectatione peccandi usque ad delectationem non peccandi indeclinabilem liberatum. Nam primum liberum arbitrium, quod homini datum est, quando primum creatus est rectus, potuit non peccare, sed potuit et peccare; hoc autem novissimum eo potentius erit, quo peccare non poterit. verum hoc quoque Dei munere, non sua possibilitate naturae. Aliud est enim, esse Deum, aliud participem Dei. Deus natura peccare non potest: particeps vero Dei ab illo accipit, ut peccare non possit." *CCL* 48,863.

9. See *De Catechizandis Rudibus* 16,24,2–4. *CCL* 46,148–9.

10. *Conf.* 8,12,29. *CSEL* 33,194–6.

11. Ibid., 1,1,1. *CSEL* 33,1.

12. Cf. *ep. Io. tr.* 4,6: "vita christiani boni, sanctum desiderium est." *PL* 35,2003.

preacher of the Gospel and the pessimism of his view of the fate of the overwhelming majority of humanity, his emphasis on love as the characteristic of Christian virtue within the Church, the Body of Christ, and his belief that those who shrink from the idea of the eternal punishment of the wicked are deceived by human good will.[13]

In considering this contrast in Augustine, it should first be remembered the degree to which he was constrained by what he accepted as orthodox Christian doctrine. Long before his day, and long afterwards, Christians accepted belief in eternal punishment for sins committed in time—Augustine devoted a chapter in *The City of God* to defending it, and another to the magnitude of Adam and Eve's disobedience as justifying the damnation of their descendants;[14] and the present repulsion from such doctrines seems to derive more from the eighteenth-century Enlightenment than from traditional Christianity. (James Joyce's conference on the torments of hell, recorded in *A Portrait of the Artist as a Young Man,* published in 1916, could have been echoed, with few modifications, though perhaps with fewer elaborations of detail, a field in which the Irish have long excelled, in many Protestant pulpits, and not only in Ireland.) The centuries-old continuing strength of the Augustinian predestinarian tradition in Western Europe and America, which includes names like Gottschalk, Bradwardine, Giles of Rome, Gregory of Rimini, Michael Baius, Calvin, Cornelius Jansen, Enrico Noris, and Jonathan Edwards, despite opposition which sometimes expressed itself in open hostility, witnesses to the attraction of the idea of the helplessness of the human soul before its creator—*Hath not the potter power over the clay, of the same lump to make one vessel unto honor and another unto dishonor?* (Rom. 9:21)—and a refusal to apply human notions of justice to God. Certainly, Augustine's doctrine encountered opposition in his own lifetime and he was driven to declare to Julian of Eclanum that unbaptized infants will suffer only the mildest pains of hell and that such suffering might be preferable to non-

13. *Ench.* 18,67. (*CCL* 46,85), where Augustine refers to *De Fide et Operibus,* esp. sections 13ff. *CSEL* 41,61ff.

14. *Civ.* 21,11. *CCL* 48,777; ibid., 14,12. *CCL* 48,433–4; cf. *ench.* 8,26–27. *CCL* 46,63–64.

existence;[15] but he continued to insist that the number of the damned greatly exceeded the number of those saved,[16] and that predestination, whether to salvation or reprobation, is absolute.[17] This teaching found general acceptance for centuries.

It is, again, necessary, in assessing his final position, to take account of the historical circumstances which affected Augustine's later thinking. The decisions of the Council of Diospolis, which initially appeared to him to endorse Pelagian doctrine, must have seemed to him to constitute a rejection, not simply of his own theology, but of the theology of African Christianity, which Augustine accepted as the theology of the universal Church. For that reason he had to press his doctrine on his fellow African bishops, who needed little persuasion, and upon the Roman see, whose theological pronouncements would have to be taken seriously in the Eastern Church.[18] In the event the Africans, supported by the weight of imperial authority, succeeded—Pelagius and Caelestius were condemned, and an ecclesiastical seal set upon their condemnation by the Council of Ephesus—even though Cyril of Alexandria was not greatly concerned with Pelagianism,[19] and apparently eventually allowed Pelagius to take refuge in Egypt.[20] The psychological shock of the verdict of Diospolis may have hardened Augustine's outlook and left him unwilling to concede anything but the bare minimum to opposition. Previous controversies with Manichaeism and Donatism had be-

15. *C. Iul.* 5,11,44. *PL* 44,809.

16. *Cor. et grat.* 10,28. *PL* 44,933.

17. *Dono pers.* 12,31; 14,35. *PL* 45,1011–2; 1014.

18. See G. Bonner, *Augustine and Modern Research on Pelagianism,* The Saint Augustine Lecture 1970, reprinted in *God's Decree and Man's Destiny* (London, 1987), no. XI; and Carole Burnett, "Dysfunction at Diospolis," *Augustinian Studies* 34 (2003): 153–73.

19. Lionel Wickham, "Pelagianism in the East," in *The Making of Orthodoxy: Essays in Honour of Henry Chadwick,* ed. Rowan Williams (Cambridge, 1989), 200–211.

20. So Eusebius, *ep.* 49 in *Collectio Avellana. CSEL* 35,114; but note the qualification of B. R. Rees: "While I cannot find any firm evidence to prove that [Pelagius] spent his last years in Egypt, I agree with J. Ferguson . . . and Wermelinger . . . that the traditional assumption that he went to Egypt from Palestine is preferable to any other" (*Pelagius: A Reluctant Heretic,* p. xii, note 13).

gun with friendly overtures and ended with bitterness; the same held true of Pelagianism: Augustine could not bear not to win.[21] In fairness it should be remembered that, for him, the issues involved the faith of the Church and human salvation.

The intellectual illumination which came upon Augustine when replying to the questions of Simplicianus of Milan was clearly a decisive factor determining his later outlook. To this should be added the conviction that, apart from martyrdom for the name of Christ,[22] only the reception of the sacrament of baptism makes salvation possible. As late as 401/2, in *De Baptismo,*[23] Augustine had been prepared to entertain Ambrose's view that faith and conversion of the heart might supply what baptism conveys,[24] but this was clearly impossible to reconcile with belief in the absolute necessity of the reception of the sacrament for salvation, and by the time of his consecration in 395, it may be guessed that he had effectively discarded it. Christ had ordained the sacrament, and whether any individual received it or not was a matter of God's disposing. Given these two unquestioned convictions, and scriptural testimony to the eternal punishment of the lost, it is understandable that Augustine's thought finalized as it did. Origen had reasoned differently; but Augustine was no Origen: he was bound by what he held to be the doctrine of the Church as defined in his own day. Furthermore, one must also take account of a genuine hardness in his mentality. His treatment

21. The same held true of his African colleagues.

22. *An. et or.* 1,9,11: "unde et latro ille non ante crucem domini sectator sed in cruce confessor, de quo nonnumquam praeiudicium captatur, sive tentatur, contra baptismatis sacramentum, a Cypriano sancto inter martyres computatur [Cyprian, *ep.* 73,22], qui suo sanguine baptizatur, quod plerisque non baptizatis fervente persecutione provenit." *CSEL* 60,311.

23. *Bapt.* 4,22,29: "baptismi sane vicem aliquando implere passionem, de latrone illo, cui non baptizato dictum est: *hodie mecum eris in paradiso,* non leve documentum idem beatus Cyprianus assumit [*ep.* 73,22]. Quod etiam atque considerans, invenio non tantum passionem pro nomine Christi id quod ex baptismo deerat posse supplere, sed etiam fidem conversionemque cordis, si forte ad celebrandum mysterium baptismi in angustiis temporum succurri non potest." *CSEL* 51,260.

24. Ambrose, *De obitu Valentiani consolatio,* 51. *PL* 16,1374.

of his concubine, which has aroused such indignation in the minds of later readers,[25] was typical of his age, and he did not rise above it.[26] In his early work, *De Ordine* (386), he accepts the necessity of the blood-stained public executioner for preserving the peace in human society.[27] Despite his painful recollection of his school-boy whippings,[28] at the end of his life he accepted the necessity of corporal punishment in a child's education.[29] He came to disapprove of capital punishment because it left no opportunity for future repentance; but he accepted the need to preserve order in human society and therefore for a man to accept the office of a judge, even though it might involve torturing an innocent person to establish the facts of a case which could, however, lead to a wrong verdict,[30] and in a famous letter to his friend Count Marcellinus, he congratulated the count for having, in a case involving Donatist violence, extracted confessions from the accused only by flogging, after which

> do not send for the executioner now that the crime has been proved, when you were not willing to employ the torturer to discover it.[31]

In short, while Augustine deplored excessive brutality he accepted conventional views of his age about the need to preserve order, in the home and in society. In modern language he was, in practice, an establishment Christian of his own day. To this may be added an indifference to the suffering of the animal creation—curious, it might be thought, in one of his sensibility—whose basis is expressed in a single sentence of the *De Natura Boni,* composed about 405: "Things which are created out of nothing, which are inferior to rational spirit, can neither be happy nor miserable."[32] The rationale had earlier been expressed in 395 in Book III of

25. *Conf.* 6,15,25. *CSEL* 33,138.

26. See Peter Brown, *Augustine of Hippo* (London, 1967), 88–90.

27. *Ord.* 2,4,12. *CCL* 29,114.

28. *Conf.* 1,9,14. *CSEL* 33,12.

29. *Civ.* 22,22,3: "pueriles poenas, sine quibus disci non potest quod maiores volunt." *CCL* 48,843.

30. Ibid., 19,6. *CCL* 48,670–71.

31. *Ep.* 133,2. *CSEL* 44,83.

32. *Nat. boni* 8.8: "Caetera vero quae sunt facta de nihilo, quae utique inferiora sunt quam spiritus rationalis, nec beata possunt esse, nec misera." *CSEL* 25/2,858.

De Libero Arbitrio: animal suffering makes clear the desire for unity in the animal body:

Were it not for the sufferings of animals we should never understand how great is the desire for [organic] unity in the lower orders of the animal kingdom; and if we did not understand that, we should not be sufficiently aware that all these things have been established by the supreme, sublime, and ineffable unity of the Creator.[33]

Animal suffering did not, in this passage at least, raise any intellectual problem for Augustine, as to how it is to be reconciled with a benevolent God—one of the major difficulties for many modern monotheists in contemplating the created order. In this, no doubt, Augustine followed an established neglect long existing in some Christian circles—*Is it for oxen that God is concerned?* asked St. Paul, when referring to the text of Deuteronomy 25:4: *You shall not muzzle the ox while it is treading out the grain. Does he not speak entirely for our sake?* (1 Cor. 9:9–10)—but it shows the anthropocentric character of his theology. Animals are part of the present order of creation, destined to pass away at the will of the Creator. They differ from man in that they lack the rational faculty which man shares with the angels,[34] which presumably explains why Augustine ignores the personal element in their suffering. Here again, it is the divine plan which matters, not the created being. It may be that Augustine's sympathy with the animal world increased with the pas-

33. *Lib. arb.* 3,23,69: "Non ergo appareret quantus inferioribus creaturis animalibus esset appetitus unitatis nisi dolore bestiarum. Quod si non appareret, minus quam opus esset admoneremur ab illa summa et sublimi et ineffabili unitate creatoris esse ista omnia constituta." *CCL* 29,316. See the comment of R. J. Teske: "Augustine's further attempts to justify to us God's way, even in the sufferings of children and animals, are valiant but far from persuasive." (*Augustine through the Ages: An Encyclopedia,* ed. A. D. Fitzgerald, 494.)

34. *Civ.* 9,13,3: ". . . homo medium quiddam est . . . inter pecora et angelos; ut quia pecus est animal irrationale, angelus autem rationale et immortale, medius homo est, inferior angelis, superior pecoribus, habens cum pecoribus mortalitatem, rationem cum angelis, animal rationale mortale." *CCL* 47,261; *ord.* 2,11.30: "Ratio est mentis motio ea, quae discuntur distinguendi et connectendi potens, qua duce uti ad deum intelligendum vel ipsam quae aut in nobis aut usquequaque est animam, rarissimum omnino genus est hominum potest, non ob aliud, nisi quia in istorum sensuum negotia progresso redire in semetipsum cuique difficile est." *CCL* 29,124.

sage of time—in *The City of God* (XIX,7) he remarked that a man would be happier in the company of his dog than with a foreigner whose language he did not understand—but his divine Creator is more a supreme Artist than a compassionate Father; and even when, in the last book of *The City of God,* he speaks enthusiastically of God's creation as a kind of indication of the beauty of heaven, he concludes by asking what will be the rewards of the blessed, when God has given such wonderful consolations to those predestined to eternal death.[35]

Yet all this is only one side of Augustine's thinking. Against it is to be set the spiritual teaching of his sermons, his eucharistic theology, with its picture of Christ, Priest and Victim, offering to the Father His Body, which is the Church,[36] and his doctrine of deification, whereby through participation in Christ the souls of human beings become as like God as it is possible for created beings to be. It would be possible to write a large book entirely omitting any reference to the doctrines which have been so severely criticized by those hostile to his theology. How are we to explain this other Augustine?

The answer is to be found in the person of Jesus Christ. In the eighth book of *The Confessions,* composed at some time between 397 and 401, Augustine describes the impression made upon him by reading the books of the Platonists, which effectively destroyed the Manichaean dualism, which had long dominated his thought, by asserting the insubstantial character of evil: it is a corruption, a lack, not a material entity as the Manichees believed. The influence of Neoplatonism on Augustine's thought was immense and long-lasting; it was to inspire Prosper Alfaric's famous theory that it was to Neoplatonism that Augustine was converted in 386 and that he only became a truly Catholic Christian a de-

35. *Civ.* 22,24. *CCL* 48,851–2.

36. See Bonner, "The Doctrine of Sacrifice: Augustine and the Latin Patristic Tradition," in *Sacrifice and Redemption: Durham Essays in Theology,* ed. S. W. Sykes (Cambridge University Press, 1991), 101–17, reprinted in *Church and Faith in the Patristic Tradition* (Aldershot: Variorum, 1996), no. XI; and "Augustine's Understanding of the Church as a Eucharistic Community," in *St. Augustine the Bishop: A Book of Essays,* ed. F. Lemoine and C. Kleinhanz (New York/London: Garland Publishing, 1994), 39–63.

cade later.[37] Few scholars maintain this theory today; most would accept the continued influence of Neoplatonism for the rest of Augustine's life, after he had confessed Christian belief and received baptism. Furthermore, belief in the God-man, Jesus Christ, was to become the foundation of Augustine's theologizing. His undergraduate reading of Cicero's *Hortensius* had inspired in him a love which lasted throughout his life, but left him unsatisfied because it lacked the name of Christ.[38] His reading of the Neoplatonists at Milan in 386 confirmed for him the truth of Christian dogma and led him to two ecstatic experiences, but convinced him that the enjoyment of God was impossible until he embraced "the mediator between God and man, the man Christ Jesus, who also is God, supreme over all things and blessed for ever,"[39] and led him to seek baptism—the vital commitment to Christianity.[40] From now on, Christ the God-man was to be at the center of Augustine's devotion, not only as the redeemer from sin, but as the sinless redeemer, by participating in whom we come to share His divinity.[41] In this sense, it can fairly be said that Augustine's spirituality is Christocentric—he takes the person and the work of Christ as the point of departure. His language does not have the tenderness found in Western medieval spirituality—this would come later[42]—but his teachings on deification and the rôle of Christ in the Eucharist: priest and victim, who offers His Body, which is the Church, have been an enduring inspiration for Christian devotion.

This does not mean that Augustine came to pass over the doctrines which have been urged against him by his critics. For example, in Sermon 111, preached in 417,[43] he explains his belief that the number of those

37. Alfaric, *L'évolution intellectuelle de saint Augustin,* Tom.I [no more published] (Paris, 1918).

38. *Conf.* 3,4,8. *CSEL* 33,48.

39. Ibid., 7,18,24. *CSEL* 33,163.

40. Ibid., 9,6,14. *CSEL* 33,207.

41. See Bonner, "Augustine's Conception of Deification," *Journal of Theological Studies,* n.s., 37 (1986): 374, reprinted in *Church and Faith in the Patristic Tradition* (Aldershot: Variorum, 1996), no. I.

42. See G. L. Prestige, *Fathers and Heretics: Six Studies in Dogmatic Faith,* with Prologue and Epilogue, Lecture 8: "Eros: Or, Devotion to the Sacred Humanity" (London, 1958), 180–207, esp. 185ff.

43. *Serm.* 111,1,1: "Certe pauli sunt qui salvantur." *PL* 38,641.

saved will be very small in comparison with those lost, basing his statement on Luke 13:24: *Strive to enter by the narrow gate,* and Matthew 7:14: *Narrow is the gate and hard the road that leads to life,* while addressing his congregation as though they would be among the saved, as he had recommended in *De dono Perseverantiae.*[44] In Sermon 27, probably preached between 397 and 401, he explains predestination as beyond human understanding with a favored quotation: *O the depth of the riches and wisdom and knowledge of God. How unsearchable are his judgments and his ways past finding out!* (Rom. 11:33–36).[45] However distasteful such views may be to later sensibilities, they are scriptural, and were not invented by Augustine.

The crucial issue remains that of Adam's sin and its effect upon his descendants. Augustine's understanding of the Fall was conditioned by his belief that Adam's offspring inherited the guilt, as well as the weakness, consequent upon the sin. This the Pelagians either denied or ignored;[46] but apart from that the Fall, in Augustine's' view, had left human beings, although made in the Image of God,[47] so weakened that they were incapable of any righteous decision, without direct divine intervention. For the Pelagians, the capacity for initiation remained, and was not destroyed by sinful actions.

Despite obvious flaws in the Pelagian psychology—habitual sin clearly does in many cases weaken the will—there is a plausibility about the Pelagian assumption which commends it to many people, as the common exhortation to "make your mind up" shows. Man may indeed be very far gone from original righteousness and is of his own fallen nature inclined to evil, but experience suggests that decisions are made, apparently by the will of the individual, of his own volition. Moreover, this accorded with the ascetic Christian tendencies of the fifth century, of which Pelagianism was an example, which sent men and women into

44. *Dono Pers.* 22,57. *PL* 45,1028.

45. *Serm.* 27,7. *CCL* 41,365–6.

46. Pelagius, in his *Commentary on Romans,* did not personally endorse anti-traducianist arguments, but simply reported them. *Pecc. mer. et rem.* 3,2,2. *CSEL* 60, 29–30.

47. *Civ.* 22,24,2. *CCL* 48,847.

the desert, to wait upon God's mercy. The desert masters of spirituality did not deny divine grace. They did, however, recognize a power in individuals, derived from God but also pertaining to man, to live righteously and so to merit grace. For Augustine, this was impossible.

The fundamental difference between Augustine and the Pelagians, then, turned on the Fall. For the Pelagians, man's nature remained fundamentally sound; for Augustine it had been corrupted to a degree which made human beings helpless of themselves to help themselves, even while he admitted—was indeed compelled by his own first principle of the anhypostatic character of evil to admit—that it could never be wholly corrupted.[48] Yet it had been weakened to such a degree as to render the sinner powerless of himself to take any step to virtue, still less to atone for the weight of inherited sin. Julian of Eclanum's accusation that Augustine remained a Manichee at heart, although a debating point, had plausibility, and the impression was accentuated by Augustine's horror of sexual concupiscence and the doctrine of the *massa peccati*.

It is pointless to speculate whether Pelagianism, if it had not been condemned, might have made a significant contribution to the spirituality of Western Christendom—we know too little of its influence upon the mass of the faithful. In pastoral practice Augustine treated men and women as having freedom of choice, whatever his deeper speculations might be. The Pelagians, on principle, took for granted a fundamental freedom and exhorted individuals to exercise it. Their theory did not commend itself to the mind of Christian devotion, but they understood the need to declare human independence of decision in the present world better than Augustine allowed. It may be that in this they had a clearer, if more limited, understanding than he. On the other hand, rigorous predestinarianism has not failed to find many supporters down the ages.

Perhaps the divergence between Augustine's high theology and his pastoral practice may be seen as inevitable, and this may be due to Augustine's Christocentricity, which affects his understanding of the rela-

48. *Vera relig.* 20,38. *CCL* 32,210; *nat. bon.* 4–6. *CSEL* 25/2,857–8; *ench.* 4,12. *CCL* 46,54.

tionship of the elect, chosen by no merit on their part but only by God's love, with their redeemer. We noticed earlier Sebastian Thier's contrast between Pelagius's and Augustine's doctrine of the Church: for Pelagius, the holiness of the Church comes from the holiness of her members; for Augustine it comes from the holiness of Christ.[49] Pelagius did not, as Augustine claimed, discount the aid of Christ, but his concern was that of the ascetic preacher: to exhort the individual Christian to strive for perfection, using the talent which God had given him. Augustine had come to disbelieve in human ability: *Without me, you can do nothing* (John 15:5).[50] For him these words were more than a theological formula; rather, they express the absolute necessity for the branches to cleave to the vine, which is Christ, who is God. Beneath Augustine's philosophical predestinarianism, there is a deeper spirituality:

> The love by which God loves us is incomprehensible and unchanging. He did not begin to love us from the time in which we were reconciled by the blood of His son, but He loved us before the foundation of the world, that we also should be His children with the Only Begotten, before we should be anything at all. . . . Therefore in a wonderful and divine way He loved us, even when He hated us, for He hated us for not being such as He had made us [because of our sins]; and because our wickedness had not wholly consumed His work, [He loved us]. He knew at one and the same time to hate in each one of us what we had done and to love what He had made.[51]

It is not easy to understand how a man who could write such language could entertain the doctrine of the *massa peccati;* but Augustine remains a theologian of paradox.

49. Thier, *Die Kirche bei Pelagius,* 322.

50. *Io. ev. tr.* 81,3: "Ne quisquam putaret saltem parum aliquem fructum posse a semetipseo palmitem ferre, cum dixisset, *hic fert fructum multum,* non ait: sine me parum potestis facere sed *nihil potestis facere;* sive ergo parum, sive multum, sine illo fieri non potest, sine quo *nihil* fieri potest." *CCL* 36,351.

51. *Io. ev. tr.* 110,6: "quapropter incomprehensibilis est dilectio, qua diligit Deus, neque mutabilis. Non enim ex quo ei reconciliati sumus per sanguinem Filii eius, nos coepit diligere: sed ante mundi constitutionem dilexit nos ut cum eius Unigenito etiam nos filii eius essemus, prius quam omnino aliquid essemus.proinde miro et divino modo et quando nos oderat, dilegebat; oderat enim nos, quales ipse non fecerat; et quia iniquitas nostra opus eius non omni ex parte consumpserat, noverat simul in unocumque nostrum et odisse quod feceramus, et amare quod fecerat." *CCL* 36,626.

John Burnaby has observed that "the attempt to extract anything like a logically consistent doctrine from the confusion of the controversy with Julian must be pronounced hopeless,"[52] while John Rist noted: ". . . there is no doubt that Augustine came to think—indeed probably always thought—that the majority of mankind, after death, will come to a bad end,"[53] which would have been a normal, though not universal, Christian assumption in his age. Augustine expresses this belief, sometimes with a disconcerting insouciance,[54] but if we are to take seriously his letter for Jerome of 415, he was far from indifferent to the fate of unbaptized infants:

> With what justice can so many thousands of souls be condemned if, being newly created, they go out of the bodies for which they were created by the will of their Creator without any preceding sin, lacking the Christian sacrament? Nor can we deny that those who leave their bodies—even tiny infants—without the sacrament of Christ go anywhere except to damnation.[55]

Yet he remained persuaded that the eternal punishment of the unbaptized was justified by the justice of a loving God, a God who took flesh for man's salvation.

One cannot, therefore, look for a system in Augustine's theology of predestination and human freedom as a whole. To the modern reader he seems able simultaneously to hold a set of incompatible principles without any reconciliation, except by the unconvincing explanation that all will be made clear at the Last Day. This is the conclusion of his letter of 418 to the monks of Hadrumetum: those who are unable to understand the mysteries of divine grace and human freedom should believe in both, as revealed truths of Scripture, and pray that they might be given understanding.[56] In view of what he had written to Jerome in 415, Augustine might well have been describing his own situation.

52. Burnaby, *Amor Dei,* 191.

53. Rist, *Augustine: Ancient Thought Baptized* (Cambridge University Press, 1994), 267.

54. *C. Iul.* 5,11,44. *PL* 44,809. cf. *ench.* 23.93. *CCL* 46,93.

55. *Ep.* 166,4,10. *CSEL* 44,560–61.

56. *Ep.* 214,7: "pray that you may also wisely understand what you piously believe." *CSEL* 57,386.

Augustine was not a theological systemizer but a rhetorician. He could expound Christian doctrine on particular issues, like the Creed, as in the *Enchiridion,* or on particular doctrines, like the Trinity, with clarity; but he never attempted to bring together his thoughts into a single system, in which every apparent contradiction was reconciled. He accepted what he believed, rightly or wrongly, to be the doctrine of the universal Church. He wrote to meet particular situations or to answer particular questions. In this way it might be suggested that compilations like the *De Diversis Quaestionibus octoginta-tribus* are particularly typical of Augustine's genius, even if not his outstanding compositions. It might have been better for posterity if, instead of answering Julian of Eclanum's six books to Florus item by item, he had produced a *summa theologiae* on Divine Grace and Human Freedom; but he did not. As a result, the modern student is left with Augustine's repetitive answers to Julian's allegations rather than with his own original thoughts.

To seek to understand the foundation of Augustine's thinking, it is useful to consider various factors conditioning his outlook during his Christian life. The first was clearly a reverence for Christ, whose name he felt he had, in a famous phrase, "drunk in with his mother's milk,"[57] so that no writing that lacked it—even Cicero's *Hortensius,* which he was to esteem throughout his life—could satisfy him. His conversion to Manichaeism did not require the renunciation of Christ's name, which the Manichees revered, but provided an explanation of the existence of evil in a world that was supposedly the work of a good Creator, a perennial problem, so far as Augustine was concerned; and it is easy to overlook the fact that, despite growing doubts, he remained a Manichee for over nine years. Furthermore, apart from the fact that Manichaean dualism for a time provided an answer to the problem of evil, the Manichees also challenged the authority of Scripture by pointing to the immoralities ascribed to various individuals and communities in the Old Testament. Au-

57. *Conf.* 3,4,8. *CSEL* 33, 49–50.

gustine's doubts were eventually set at rest by the sermons of Ambrose: not everything was to be taken literally.[58] However, Ambrose made it clear that certain truths had to be believed without demonstration[59] and this principle remained fixed in Augustine's mind. Some scriptural teachings had to be taken literally, among them being the texts *Many are called but few chosen*[60] and *Unless you eat the flesh of the Son of Man and drink his blood you have no life in you.*[61] Augustine eventually ceased to be a Manichee; but the effect of his rejection of his Manichaean decade remained with him throughout his Catholic life.

The final destruction of Manichaean influence on Augustine was brought about by his reading of the Neoplatonists, who persuaded him of the insubstantiality of evil, and no one will question the continued influence of Neoplatonism on Augustine's thinking; but did it influence Augustine's views on predestination? Peter Brown had implied so. "Far above the sunlit surface of Julian's Bible, the God of Augustine had remained the ineffable God of the Neo-Platonic mystic,"[62] but that is not the impression given, at least to the present writer, by reading, for example, Sermon 27 on Psalm 95 and on Romans 9:15: *I will have mercy on whom I will have mercy and I will have compassion on whom I will have compassion:*

> Are you, perhaps, expecting me to tell you why He has mercy on whom He will and whom He will He hardens? Are you expecting it from me, a man? If you are a man and I am a man, then both of us have heard: *O man, who are you to an-*

58. Ibid., 6,3,4–5,7. *CSEL* 33, 117–21.

59. Ibid., 6,5,7: "ex hoc tamen quoque iam praeponens doctrinam catholicam, modestius ibi minimeque falliciter sentiebam iuberi, ut crederetur quod non demonstrabatur—sive esset quid, sed cui forte non esset, sive nec quid esset—quam illic temeraria pollicitatione scientiae credulitatem inrideri et postea tam multa fabulosissima et absurdissima, qui demonstrati non poterant, credenda imperari." *CSEL* 33,120.

60. *Serm.* 111,1: "Pauci ergo qui salvantur in comparatione multorum periturorum." *PL* 38,642.

61. *C. duas. epp. Pel.* 1,22,40; 2,4,7; cf. 4,4,8: "haec reconciliatio est in lavacro regenerationis et Christi carne et sanguine, sine quo nec parvuli possunt habere vitam in semet ipsis." *CSEL* 60,457–8; 467; 529.

62. Brown, *Augustine of Hippo,* 393.

swer back to God? So trusting ignorance is better than rash knowledge. God says to me, Christ speaks through the apostle, *O man, who are you to answer back to God?*[63]

The reference to Christ may here be significant, for it was precisely the absence of Christ's name from the Neoplatonist writings at Milan which left Augustine dissatisfied in 385. He attempted—and to some degree succeeded—two ascents of the mind to God.[64] They were of a very intellectual character and the second closely paralleled the description of the ascent of the mind to God which he had described in *De Quantitate Animae* of 387/388,[65] in which he noted the rejection by the Neoplatonists of the Christian doctrine of the Incarnation.[66] However, in *The Confessions* he specifically declared that he felt that he needed a strength, not his own, to enjoy God, and only found it when he embraced *"the mediator between God and man, the man Christ Jesus, who is also God over all, blessed for ever."*[67] *The Confessions* were written a decade or more after the *De Quantitate Animae.* Significantly, the quotation from 1 Timothy 2:5 speaks of Christ, the Mediator between God and man, the conception which plays so important a part in Augustine's theology,[68] while of the *De Quantitate Animae* it has been said that in its depiction of the seven degrees of the ascent of the mind to God it shows real Neoplatonic influence, with corrections inspired by the sharpened sense of the Christian convert, to provide a doctrine of enduring value.[69]

The *De Quantitate Animae* provides, in its discussion of the ascent of the soul, to be paralleled a decade later in *The Confessions* 7,17,23, an early example of the way in which Augustine draws upon, and Christian-

63. *Serm.* 27,4. *CCL* 41,362–3. Tr. by Hill, slightly modified.

64. See Bonner, "Augustine and Mysticism," in *Augustine: Mystic and Mystagogue,* ed. F. van Fleteren, J. C. Schnaubelt, and Joseph Reino (New York, 1994), 129–35.

65. See F. Cayré, *La contemplation augustinienne* (Paris, 1925), 69–76.

66. *Quant. an.* 33,76. *CSEL* 89, 223–5; cf. *civ.* 10,29,1. *CCL* 47,304.

67. *Conf.* 7,18,24: "Et quarebam viam comparandi roboris, quod esset idoneum ad fruendum te, nec inveniebam, donec amplecterer *mediatorem dei et hominum, hominem Christum Iesum, qui est super omnia, deus benedictus in secula* (1 Tim. 2:5), vocantem et dicentem: *Ego sum via, veritas et vita* (Ioh 14:6)." *CSEL* 33,163.

68. See note 41 above.

69. Cayré, *La contemplation augustinienne,* see note 65 above.

izes, Neoplatonic concepts. An excellent example of this is found in his use of the doctrine of participation, expressed in *De Diversis Quaestionibus 83,* where he identifies the Platonic Ideas as thoughts in the mind of God and declares that it is by participating in them that every created being exists;[70] and in the twenty-third *Tractate on the Gospel of John* (414) he writes:

> This is the Christian religion, that one God is to be worshipped, and not many gods, because the soul is not made blessed except by one God. It is made blessed by participation in God. The weak soul is not made blessed by participation in a holy soul, nor is a holy soul made blessed by participation in an angel; but if the weak soul seeks to be made blessed, let it seek that by which the holy soul is made blessed. You yourself are not made blessed by an angel, but from whence an angel is made blessed, thence are you also. With these truths most firmly established in advance: that the reasonable soul is not made blessed except by God, and the body not animated except by the soul, and that the soul is a kind of middle term between God and the body, direct your thoughts and remember with me . . . and let us delve with all our powers until we come to the rock: Christ the Word, Christ the Word of God with God, the Word Christ and God the Word, Christ and God and the Word one God. . . . But not only was the Word Christ, but the Word was made flesh and dwelt among us. Therefore Christ is both Word and flesh.[71]

Tractate 23 emphasizes the divinity and humanity of Jesus Christ, conjoined in one Person, which makes Him the Mediator between God and man, by whom the elect come to blessedness, which is deification. Augustine declares in a sermon:

> The teacher of humility and sharer of our infirmity, giving us participation in His divinity, coming down that He might both teach and be the Way, has deigned most highly to commend His humility to us.[72]

It can be said that the conception of Christ the Mediator, God made man, is central to Augustine's evangelical teaching. "He has been made weak that we might be strong."

70. *Div. quaest. LXXXIII,* q. 46,2. *CCL* 44 A, 72–73.
71. *Io. ev. tr.* 23,5–6. *CCL* 36,235.
72. *En. Ps. 58, serm.* 1,7. *CCL* 38,734.

> We too are made by His grace what we were not, that is, Sons of God. Yet we were something else, and that much inferior, that is sons of men. Therefore He descended that we might ascend, and remaining in His nature was made a partaker of our nature, that we remaining in our nature might be made partakers of His nature. But not simply thus; for His participation in our nature did not make Him worse, while participating in His nature makes us better.[73]

Devotion to Christ's flesh-taking as the action which saves fallen humanity was therefore central to Augustine's theology; but he went further: human salvation deifies: "To make gods those who were men, He was made man who is God."[74] The great vision embodied in this declaration—the elevation of the fallen created being to adoption by the Creator, already taking place in hope within the fellowship of the Christian Church, Christ's Body, to be perfected in the General Resurrection—seems to be so utterly different in spirit from Augustine's theology of predestination and Original Sin as to justify Thomas Allin's reference to "two distinct theologies" in his writings: the earlier one, due to "the Catholic traditions," which Augustine at first accepted with little question; the other due to "the maturer workings of his mind."[75] Nevertheless Augustine continues to speak of deification, even when the stream of anti-Pelagian writings between 411–12 and his death was absorbing much of his energy and causing him to emphasize predestination rather than participation.

The interpretation of Augustine's later doctrinal outlook is made more difficult by the part which concupiscence plays in his theology of Original Sin,[76] which Julian of Eclanum was to denounce, and which has

73. *Ep.* 140,4,10: ". . . nos quoque per eius gratiam facti sumus, quod non eramus, id est filii dei, sed tamen aliquid eramus, et hoc ipsum multo inferius, hoc est filii hominum. descendit ergo ille, ut nos ascenderemus, et manens in sua natura factus est particeps naturae nostrae, ut nos manentes in natura nostra efficeremur participes naturae ipsius, non tamen sic; nam illum naturae nostrae participatio non fecit deteriorem, nos autem facit naturae illius participatio meliores." *CSEL* 44,162.

74. *Serm.* 192,1,1: "facturus deos qui homines erant, homo factus est qui deus erat." *PL* 38,1012.

75. Allin, *The Augustinian Revolution in Theology,* 107–8.

76. See the articles by G. Bonner, *Augustinus Lexikon,* vol. 1, fasc. 7/8, 1114–22, and Peter Burnell, in *Augustine through the Ages: An Encyclopedia,* 224–7.

revolted the feelings of more recent students like Allin.[77] It is clear that encratite tendencies appeared early in Christian morality and were encouraged by the rise and triumph of monasticism. To this general tendency may be added a personal factor: Augustine's experience of the power of sexual desire at the time of his conversion at Milan. He did not, however, have the revulsion from sexuality displayed by Jerome in his attack on Jovinian, and in the *De Bono Coniugali* defended the institution of Christian marriage, while setting celibacy on a higher level. The appeal made by his understanding of concupiscence, as evidence of the loss by human beings of the ability which existed in Eden to control the action of their genitals—physiologically erroneous but psychologically persuasive in its day—and the repeated challenges to this view by Julian of Eclanum, caused him to dwell all too abundantly upon the topic. In itself, however, the fact that concupiscence witnessed to an inherited guilt seems to have been a debating point for him rather than a preoccupation.

Equally Augustine spoke of deification, a doctrine which was to be found in Christian theology both in the East and the West,[78] to emphasize the glories of the work of human redemption by Christ, the Word made flesh and the Mediator between God and man. However, in considering the mass of humanity, Augustine took literally the words of the Bible: not all are saved. His conviction that God's will cannot be frustrated explained his determination to maintain that the words of 1 Timothy 2:4: *God our Savior, who desires all men to be saved and to come to a knowledge of the truth* cannot be accepted as they stand, but must be explained away.[79] Augustine may be accused of quibbling; but the need to explain difficult passages of Scripture which do not harmonize with the understanding of the whole easily leads to quibbling.

77. Allin, *Augustinian Revolution,* 141: "Sex and sin are . . . two watchwords of Augustinianism, two pillars of its temple."

78. In the West Augustine had been anticipated by Irenaeus, *Adversus Haereses,* and by Novatian, *De Trinitate.*

79. *Ench.* 27,103. *CCL* 46,104–6; *c. Iul.* 4,4,42. *PL* 44,759; *cor. et grat.* 14,44; 15,47. *PL* 44, 943; 945.

In the last resort, Augustine's formulation of Original Sin as conveying guilt to the human race represents a decisive development of earlier understandings of the doctrine; but it is an explanation and attempted justification of the ways of God to men, and does not alter the essential doctrine that ultimately election and reprobation are determined by God's will, which is a mystery.

The failure, a failure not uncommon among apologists, was that having proclaimed the mystery, Augustine then sought to defend it by argument. Julian of Eclanum urged that divine justice could not be fundamentally different from the human understanding of its character.[80] Augustine pointed to the Psalm: *You thought unjustly that I was like you* (Ps. 49 [50]:21), and urged that the child who dies in infancy, unbaptized, is justly excluded from heaven as a punishment for inherited sin.[81] The modern reader is not likely to be impressed, even by the assurance that the pains of such damnation are the mildest of all,[82] or that their final state is preferable to non-existence.[83] Dreadful as this view seems to be, it must be seen in the circumstances of the later patristic period, when a theologian as optimistic as Gregory of Nyssa could issue a warning to those who defer baptism.[84] That Augustine's statements were destined to have a dominating effect upon later Western theology cannot be doubted. That his views were necessarily shocking to the majority of believers in the fifth century is more open to question. It has already been suggested that Augustine in many matters was more conventional and more in

80. *Op. imp.* 2,80–84; 3,5–9. *CSEL* 85/1, 219–21; 353–5.

81. Ibid., 3, 9: "IUL.: 'There could be someone who thinks that what he does not see does not exist, but there has never been found anyone who said that what he believed to be divine is unjust.' AUG.: 'You yourself are found to be such a person. For to whom, if not to such as you, does Scripture say: *You thought unjustly that I was like you?* (Ps. 49 [50]; 21). But since Catholic Christians both know that God exists and that He is just, they cannot doubt that, if human beings who have been born in infancy without being reborn, even though they are images of God, they are not taken into the Kingdom of God, and that this is not unjust, but a punishment for Original Sin.'" *CSEL* 85/1,355. Tr. by R. J. Teske.

82. *Pecc. mer. et rem.* 1,16,21. *CSEL* 60,20; *ench.* 23,93. *CCL* 46,99.

83. *Ep.* 184A, 2. *CSEL* 44,733.

84. Greg. Nyss., *Adversus eos qui differunt baptismum. PG* 46, 416C–432, esp. 424C–425B.

harmony with the tendencies of his age than is easily assumed—an example would be his acceptance in later life of miracles worked by relics of the saints, recorded in *The City of God* Book XXII; but there are other cases which anticipate later practices: the demon-infested farm at Zubedi, in the district of Fussala, which was exorcised when one of Augustine's presbyters celebrated a Eucharist there,[85] or the even more startling anticipation of medieval piety in the account told to Julian of Eclanum—of all people—of how a certain Acatius, born with his eyelids joined together, was cured without an operation by his pious mother, who caused a poultice made from the bread of the Eucharist to be placed upon them.[86] It may be that Augustine's anti-Pelagian theology did in fact command considerable popular support as well as imperial backing.

85. *Civ.* 22,8,6. *CCL* 48,820.

86. *Op. imp.* 3,162. *CSEL* 85/1,467–8. Julian had argued that the work of God in the newly born has no need of correction. Augustine cited the case of Acatius to refute him. Julian, however, was concerned with the moral state of the infant, while Augustine cites a physical blemish, which could be ascribed to the effects of the Fall. The episode seems amazingly superstitious, but hardly more so than the case of Ambrose's brother, Satyrus, who, being yet unbaptized, was preserved in a shipwreck, having a portion of the consecrated host bound round his neck in a napkin (Ambrose, *De Excessu Satyri,* 1,43. *PL* 16,1304).

CHAPTER 7

CONCLUSION

THE DOCTRINES which Augustine asserted against the Pelagians were formulated long before the controversy began. There is no good reason to doubt his assertion of the decisive effect upon him of the intellectual illumination which occurred when he was writing to Simplicianus of Milan in about 397, in which divine grace triumphed over human initiative and freedom of choice. The notion of the *massa* or lump of sin, such a decisive issue in the controversy, appears as Question 68 of *De diversis Quaestionibus octoginta-tribus,* published in 395/6, and must therefore be earlier than that date. So far as Augustine was concerned, he was persuaded that the essence of his anti-Pelagian theology had been expressed in the *Ad Simplicianum,* this claim being repeated in the *De Praedestinatione Sanctorum*[1] and in the *De dono Perseverantiae,* where he wrote: "I began to have a fuller knowledge of this truth [viz., that divine grace is given by God's gratuitous mercy and not by any preceding merits on our part] in that treatise which I wrote for Simplicianus of happy memory, the bishop of Milan, at the beginning of my episcopate, when I realized and stated that the beginning of faith is also the gift of God."[2] Furthermore, at some time after 400 he abandoned the view, inherited from St. Ambrose, that where the opportunity of baptism was lacking, faith and the conversion of the heart

1. *Praed. sanct.* 4,8. *PL* 44,966, quoting *retract.* 2,1 [27/28]. *CCL* 57,89–90.
2. *Dono Pers.* 20,52. *PL* 45, 1026. Tr. Teske.

might suffice.[3] From henceforth, martyrdom apart, there was no possibility of salvation for the unbaptized. In the *De Peccatorum Meritis et Remissione,* his first anti-Pelagian writing, significantly subtitled *On Infant Baptism,* he emphasized this.[4] Thus by 411, Augustine's views were fully formed. They would become harsher in the course of controversy, but not altered.

The Pelagian case was different. They were not a united group with a commonly formulated theology, except in their assumption of human freedom. From Rufinus of Syria, a somewhat shadowy figure,[5] they inherited a general hostility to traducianism, of which Caelestius was the spokesman, judging from his trial at Carthage in 411. Pelagius, although he recorded arguments against any transmission of Original Sin in his commentary on Romans,[6] does not seem to have had Caelestius's interest in the matter. It is possible—but can only be a hypothesis—that their parting in Africa in 411 and Pelagius's departure for Jerusalem could have been inspired by disagreement about Caelestius's aggressively anti-traducian teaching. It may be significant that at his trial at Diospolis Pelagius emphatically disassociated himself from certain propositions ascribed to his former ally: "Let those who say that these are Caelestius's statements see whether they are Caelestius's or not. I, however, never held them, and I declare anathema anyone who holds them."[7] This could

3. *De Baptismo* 4,22,29. *CSEL* 51,257; Ambrose, *De obitu Valentiani consolatio,* 51. *PL* 16,1374.

4. *Pecc. mer. et rem* 1,16,21. *CSEL* 60,20.

5. See Bonner, "Rufinus of Syria and African Pelagianism," *Augustinian Studies* 1 (1970): 31–47, reprinted in *God's Decree and Man's Destiny* (London, 1987), no X; Henri Marrou, "Les attaches orientales du Pélagianisme," Comptes Rendus de l'Académie des Inscriptions & Belles-Lettres (1968), 459–72; Eugene TeSelle, "Rufinus the Syrian, Caelestius, Pelagius: Explorations in the Prehistory of the Pelagian Controversy," *Augustinian Studies* 3 (1972): 61–95. Rufini Presbyteri, *Liber de Fide,* critical text and translation with introduction and commentary by Sister Mary William Miller, The Catholic University of America Patristic Studies, vol. 96 (Washington, D.C., 1984).

6. Pelagius, *Expositiones XII epistularum Paul,* ed. A. Souter: Ad Romanos 5;15. *PLS* 1,1137; *pecc. mer. et rem.* 3,2,2. *CSEL* 60,129.

7. *Gest. Pel.* 14,30. *CSEL* 42, 84.

be evidence of a coolness between the two men—Pelagius made no effort to defend his absent friend. Caelestius was subsequently to seek to vindicate Pelagius's reputation as well as his own; but any question of friendship apart, it was obviously in his own interest to do so. They had been condemned together and it would be to their joint advantage to be cleared together, since this would amount to papal endorsement of the orthodoxy of their teaching.

Though Pelagius may or may not have regarded acceptance or denial of the doctrine of Original Sin as a major theological issue, its implications determined the Pelagian Controversy, inasmuch as it affected the understanding of the power of human nature after the Fall. Augustine was convinced that the Fall had so corrupted the human will that it necessitated a specific impulse of divine grace for every righteous human action, however trivial, even after baptism, so that even the saintliest persons to the end of their lives needed to pray *deliver us from evil.*[8] For Pelagians of any and every variety, the individual had a residue of the initiative, given by God in creation, which enabled him to choose to act righteously. For Augustine, this amounted to a claim to be independent of God; but it need not have been so, but only an assertion that the God-given freedom of choice in the will had not been so weakened by sin, inherited or personal, that it could only choose to do evil unless assisted by an immediate impulsion of grace for every good action. The weakness of the Pelagian position was an undervaluation of the effect on the will by long-continued sinning. The weakness of the Augustinian was the assumption of an inherited corruption which seemed to make nonsense of his fundamental belief in the goodness of God's creation. From the Pelagian standpoint, a baptized person ought to be able to refrain from sin: he now had it in his power. Their attitude resembled that of St. Cyprian after his baptism, recorded in the *Ad Donatum*. Augustine's position was more realistic: baptism removes inherited guilt, but human

8. *C. duas epp. Pel.* 4,10.27. *CSEL* 60,556–7.

nature, weakened by the Fall, needs to be healed by a lifetime's convalescence, which is only perfected after death.[9]

Pelagian theology, assuming as it does human freedom, naturally assumes individual responsibility: we have the power to act righteously and if we fail to do so we deserve to be punished, and will be punished in hellfire. Augustine's attitude was more complicated, because of his notion of an inherited guilt which automatically damns us. This guilt can be removed only by baptism or martyrdom. However, baptism does not restore us to the state of unfallen Adam in Paradise, who had a freedom of choice, which he abused. Adam certainly had need of God's grace in Eden before the Fall,[10] but he was free in a way that his descendants are not: he could choose whether he would do good or evil: his offspring could only do evil, unless empowered by God's unmerited grace. Can we therefore say that they have liberty of choice in any real sense of the word? Augustine expressed his understanding in his letter to Firmus: God provided the grace for every individual good decision in advance, and the individual who used it made a free choice; but God, in His inscrutable wisdom, might withhold the grace from some persons. Can one, in such circumstances, say that the individual is truly free? The Pelagian view, which accepts that man owes his being to God the Creator and that he has a subsisting God-given choice between good and evil, what Julian called "emancipation from God," seems more in accordance with human experience in this life than does Augustine's, even if it does not take account of failures due to inherited weakness and long-continued habit. On the other hand, Augustine's recognition of the turbulence and division in the human mind, what he understands by concupiscence in a wider sense than simply the sexual, has a psychological significance which goes deeper than the simpler assumptions of Pelagian thinking.

To this may be added Augustine's sense of a desire for God which

9. *Gn. litt.* 6,24,35. *CSEL* 28/1,196–7.

10. The *adiutorium sine quo non;* see *cor. et grat.* 11,31–32; 12,34; 38. *PL* 44,935; 936–7; 939–40.

persists in human beings even after the Fall, though it may be obscured by the desire for lower, created goods rather than for their Creator. Augustine accepts that the desire for happiness is part of human nature; but it is much more than a conscious desire: it is the natural condition of humanity, disastrously damaged by Adam's sin but destined to be restored in the elect and, indeed, to be raised to new heights through participation in the divine nature, not through any merits on the part of the individual but by God's infinite mercy. The problem for Augustine is that God is both a God of mercy and a God of justice, and the Bible makes it clear that the lost, according to Scripture, deserve their fate: *Depart from me you cursed into hell fire* (Matt. 25:41)—a text quoted by Augustine[11]—in striking agreement with the words of Pelagius: "In the day of judgment the wicked and sinners are not to be spared; rather they are to be burned with eternal fires."[12] "Augustine would agree with the Aristotle of the *Poetics* that there is nothing tragic (or regrettable) in seeing an evil man getting his deserts."[13] The moral difficulty is that many infants get their deserts from nothing other than lack of baptism and an inherited guilt over which they have had no control. God has made them for Himself—and yet rejects them with inscrutable justice. *And when I am lifted up from the earth, I will draw everyone after me* (John 12:32). But Augustine's text did not read *omnes,* "everyone," but *omnia,* "all things" (= *omnia genera*).

Therefore, when He said: *Now is the prince of this world cast out and I, if I am lifted up from the earth, will draw* omnia *after me*—why *omnia,* except from the things which He has cast out, *for not all have faith?* (2 Thess. 3:2). Therefore He does not refer to the entirety of humanity, but to the wholeness of created beings, that is spirit and mind and body, namely to that by which we understand and live and are visible and tangible. For He who said: *Not a hair of your heads shall perish* (Luke 21:18) *draws all things after Him.* But if by *omnia* human beings are to be understood, we can say "all who are predestinated to salvation," of whom none shall perish, as He said earlier of His sheep (John 10:28). Cer-

11. *Op. imp.* 6,31,2. *CSEL* 85/2,424.
12. *Gest. Pel.* 3,9. *CSEL* 42,60; Hieron., *Dial. con. Pel.* 1,28. *PL* 23,544.
13. Rist, *Augustine: Ancient Thought Baptized,* 273.

tainly all races of men, of all tongues and races, or of all ranks and of all varieties or abilities, or of all lawful and useful occupations, and whatever else may be mentioned by which human beings differ among themselves, sins only excepted, from the highest to the lowest, from the king to the beggar, *omnia,* He says, *I will draw after me,* so that He may be their head and they His members.[14]

Once more Augustine insists that not all are saved, using the same arguments that he used to explain away 1 Timothy 2:4 in the *Enchiridion.*[15] Yet there is another aspect of Augustine's thinking, expressed in the great outburst: "Late have I loved Thee, beauty so old and so new, late have I loved Thee."[16] Augustine conceives of an instinct for God implanted in mankind which is part of human nature. Humanity aspires to God, drawn by the divine loveliness. This aesthetic aspect of Augustine's thought has deservedly been the object of much study in recent years.[17] It is less an ascent of the mind to God by the will of the mystic than the attraction of love of the beautiful, to be related to grace rather than to will. Augustine complicates the matter in *The Confessions* by the strange question: "What am I to You, that you command me to love You, and unless I do are angry with me and threaten me with huge miseries?"[18] Can one command love, as opposed to fear or obedience, under the threat of punishment? Or is Augustine here so affected by the notion of the divine beauty, that the threatened punishment is simply the necessary consequence of refusing to behold it? Punishment for disobedience can be understood, but can one logically be punished for a failure in loving?

> They wilfully themselves exile from light
> And must for aye consort with endless night.

14. *Ioh. ev. tr.* 52,11. *CCL* 36,450.

15. *Ench.* 27,103. *CCL* 46,104–6.

16. *Conf.* 10,27,38. *CSEL* 33,255.

17. E.g., R. J. O'Connell, *Art and the Christian Intelligence in St. Augustine* (Cambridge, Mass., 1978/Oxford: Basil Blackwell, 1978); Carol Harrison, *Beauty and Revelation in the Thought of St. Augustine* (Oxford: Oxford University Press, 1992); J.-M. Fontanier, *La Beauté selon St. Augustin* (Presses Universitaires de Rennes, 1998); Michael Hanby, *Augustine and Modernity* (London/New York, 2003).

18. *Conf.*1,5,5. *CSEL* 33,4.

Augustine understands this clearly enough in Sermon 178:

> . . . if you are longing to see your God, if during this exile, this wandering, you are sighing for love of Him, why then, the Lord your God is testing you, as if He were to say to you: "Look, do what you like, satisfy all your greedy desires, extend the scope of your wickedness, give free rein to your self-indulgence, consider as lawful whatever happens to please you; I won't punish you for any of this, I won't cast you into hell; I will just deny you the sight of my face." If that has horrified you, then you have really loved. If your heart shuddered at what has just been said: that your God will deny you the sight of his face, it means you accounted not seeing your God as a terrible punishment; it means you have loved freely.[19]

The consequence of this notion of a continuing desire for God in the human soul would appear to conflict with Augustine's parallel assumption of a major corruption, a notion which was developed by some later followers into a theology of a total depravity, but which does not harmonize with his dogmatic insistence elsewhere on the anhypostatic quality of evil. Nevertheless, while Julian of Eclanum's charge that Augustine had remained a Manichee at heart was unfair, Augustine's emphasis on the power of evil in a fallen world understandably seems to many to be extravagant, unless we remember the miseries of the world and still more the wickedness perpetrated by individuals and groups throughout the course of human history. While most men and women never commit serious sins in the course of their lifetimes, others—and they are not necessarily monsters—will sometimes participate in major crimes at the orders of authority or by personal appetite. There is a mystery in human wickedness, which in ordinary circumstances seems inexplicable; yet the perpetrators are often ordinary men and in many cases do collectively what they would not do as individuals.

The dramatic contrast between the Augustinian and Pelagian theologies has meant that they have commonly been regarded as absolute-

19. *Serm.* 178,9,10–10,11. *PL* 38,966. Tr. Hill. Cf. *ep. Io. tr.* 4,6: "Tota vita christiani boni sanctum desiderium est. Quod autem desideras, nondum vides; sed desiderando capax efficeris, ut cum venerit, quod videas, implearis. . . . Tantum autem nos exercet sanctum desiderium, quantum desideria nostra amputaverimus ab amore saeculi." *PL* 35,2009–10.

ly opposed and irreconcilable, while within Augustine's own thought is the paradox of his insistence that man, though disastrously fallen, still bears the marks of his heavenly creation, and the promise, for some, of divinization, of an elevation by the grace of God through the Incarnation to a higher condition than Adam enjoyed in Paradise. For centuries, Pelagianism was denounced as the worst of heresies because it was held to teach that man is independent of God. Yet the notion of creation from nothing, which the Pelagians did not deny, means that the source of human power to act righteously is, and can only be, God, who has bestowed the choice between good and evil action upon man. The doctrine of the Fall need not necessarily destroy all freedom of choice, as Augustine assumed; it may only make right-doing more difficult. It was the denial of such freedom, except for wrongdoing, in Augustine's mature thinking[20] which provoked the opposition of the so-called Semi-Pelagians; but was their opposition necessarily heretical? Augustine assumed so, and so have his descendants, from Gottschalk to the divines of the Synod of Dort; but his own predestinarian theology is not a doctrine of the universal Church, and would be rejected by many who equally reject Pelagianism and denounce it, unfairly, as a shallow and rationalistic theology. Carried to an extreme, however, the consequences of Augustine's doctrine of predestination produce a system which comes close to that of James Hogg's *Confessions of a Justified Sinner* and is parodied by Vincent of Lérins in his *Commonitorum:*

> They dare to promise and to teach that in their Church—that is in the little assembly of their communion—there is a certain special and wholly personal grace of God, that without any labor or effort or diligence, even if they do not seek or find or knock (cf. Matt. 7:7), whoever belong to their number are so protected by divine grace that they can never *dash their feet against a stone* (Matt. 4:6), so that, being *borne up on angelic hands* (cf. Matt. 4:11)—that is, preserved by angelic protection—they shall never be made to stumble (cf. Rom. 14:21).[21]

20. *C. duas ep. Pel.* 1,2,4; 3,7; 2,5,9. *CSEL* 60,125; 428–9; 468–9; *grat. et lib. arb* 8,20. *PL* 44,892–4.

21. *Commonitorium* 26: "Audent etenim polliceri et doceri, quod in ecclesia sua, id est in communionis suae conventiculo, magna et specialis ac plane personalis quaedam sit

Whether these words are directed against Augustine's predestinarian theology or not, and the suggestion has been questioned, they can be understood as a criticism of unconditional election to grace.[22]

Pelagian thinking has been criticized on three main counts. First, that it denies any internal enabling grace, as opposed to grace of illumination and baptism. This was Augustine's charge. It has been argued that this is unfair:[23] Pelagius argued that the power to do good was of God, and it was not necessary for Adam's descendants to have lost it completely in this world as the result of Adam's sin. The Pelagian argument was that power still subsists in the individual, if he or she cares to exercise it. It is not clear that this principle should, in itself, be judged heretical. It would be heretical—and absurd—if it were claimed that the individual does not need God's aid; but this was not the Pelagian claim. What they did urge was that God gave the power and freedom of choice and would judge its exercise. For Augustine the matter was more complicated. On his own first principles he denied that, since the Fall, the individual had any freedom of choice, except to sin. In addition, the individual was involved in the common guilt in Adam's primal sin, for which he deserved damnation, even if he added nothing to it—hence the fate of unbaptized infants. According to this reasoning the individual cannot fairly be held responsible for his actions. In practice Augustine's thinking would hold him responsible, even though he had no opportunity to avoid sinning.

Secondly, even accepting that Pelagius did admit grace, it may be maintained that his conception was inadequate,[24] that he conceived it

---

dei gratia, adeo ut sine ullo labore sine ullo studio, sine ulla industria, etiamsi nec petant nec quaerant nec pulsent, quicumque illi ad numerum suum pertinent, tamen ita divinitus dispensentur, ut angelicis avecti manibus, id est angelica protectione servati, numquam possint offendere *ad lapidem pedem suum,* id est, numquam scandalizari." *PL* 50,674.

22. See Rebecca Hardin Weaver, *Divine Grace and Human Agency* (Macon, Ga., 1996), 158: "Vincent did not mention Augustine by name but he assailed a distorted version of Augustine's teaching that an otherwise unidentified group or sect was propagating."

23. See above, Introduction and chapters 4 and 6.

24. So Robert F. Evans, *Pelagius: Inquiries and Reappraisals* (New York, 1968), 111.

only in terms of enlightenment, in law and doctrine, and in the remission of sins in baptism.[25] Pelagian theology, as we have it, lacked Augustine's emphasis on the mediation of Christ and the life-giving indwelling of the Holy Spirit in the soul,[26] and Augustine in 418 brutally dismissed Pelagius's belated confession that the grace of God was necessary, not only for every hour and every moment, but for every individual action of our lives[27]—much the same language as Augustine himself was to use to Firmus at a later date. There is a case for suspecting that in 418 Augustine was determined to ensure that Pelagius was condemned in order to vindicate his own orthodoxy.

Thirdly, it can be maintained that Pelagianism led to the sin of pride. This is a theme of Augustine's treatise *On the Grace of the New Testament:* the foolish virgins symbolize those Christians who put their trust in their own virtues and do good for human praise.[28] Clearly, there is such a danger in Pelagianism, an ascetic movement with the temptation of such movements for the ascetic to take pride in his own achievements, and it was a weakness of which Augustine was very conscious; but it would be unjust to accuse Pelagius and his supporters of deliberately encouraging vanity. Certainly, the aristocratic character of Roman Pelagianism ensured that proper respect was given to social status, and Pelagius reminded the virgin Demetrias that she came of the famous Anician family;[29] but he urged that her nobility should be transferred to her soul, which ought to be ashamed to be enslaved by vices. It may be added that so forceful an anti-Pelagian as St. Jerome had an appropriate respect for rank, and worth remembering that the Jansenists were very far from being free of snobbery.[30] In short, Pelagianism was characteristic of its age and ethos: an aristocratic, ascetic Christian movement, with the hauteur

25. See Torgny Bohlin, *Die Theologie des Pelagius und ihre Genesis* (Uppsala/Wiesbaden, 1957), 15–45.

26. *Sp. et litt.* 21,36; 28,48. *CSEL* 60,189; 202–3.

27. *Grat. Christ. et pecc. orig.* 1,2,2. *CSEL* 42,125–6.

28. *Ep.* 140, 31,74–75. *CSEL* 44,221–4.

29. Pelagius, *Ad Demetriaden* 22. *PL* 30,37–8; 33,1114.

30. Ronald Knox, *Enthusiasm: A Chapter in the History of Religion* (Oxford, 1950), 176–203.

and exclusiveness which goes with it.[31] Like other Christian movements throughout history, it had its weaknesses, but that discredits it only to the degree that perfection is impossible in this life.

What can be said in favor of Pelagianism is that it emphasized the responsibility of the individual for his actions in the eyes of God, because it either rejected or minimized the legacy of Original Sin.[32] Augustine also emphasized responsibility, but it is difficult to see how, on his first premises, the individual can avoid sin without a specific gift of grace to enable him to do so, which means that man is simply God's instrument. While in the last analysis it may be felt that Augustine's understanding of the action of God upon the human soul goes deeper than the simpler psychology of Pelagius, Caelestius, and Julian, it is possible to feel that their attempt to defend human initiative deserved more consideration than it received in its day and in later ages.

The Pelagian Controversy is commonly deemed the major theological debate in the Western Church in the patristic period, and continued to arouse controversy for centuries. The Reformation revived passions on both the Protestant and Catholic sides. Given the momentous consequences of the Pelagian affair, it is remarkable how fortuitous was the sequence of events which led to the crisis of 418.[33] If Caelestius had gone to Palestine with Pelagius in 411 and not remained in Africa to be attacked by Paulinus of Milan (not an African); if Orosius had not so mishandled the case for the prosecution at Jerusalem in 415; if Augustine had been less concerned for his reputation after the acquittal of Pelagius at the Synod of Diospolis; if his African colleagues had been less concerned to vindicate their unuttered assumption that what Africa maintains today the universal Church will think tomorrow, histo-

31. Julian of Eclanum had to the full the aristocratic sense of superiority.

32. See J. K. Mozley, *A Treatise on Augustinian Predestination*, 3rd ed. (London, 1883), 49: "This is the explanation of the Pelagian grace, as *Lex et Natura*, which we meet so often in St. Augustine. But with all deference to so great a name, I cannot think that this adverse explanation is altogether justified by the language of the Pelagians themselves."

33. See Bonner, "Pelagianism Reconsidered," *Studia Patristica* 27 (1993): 237–41, reprinted in *Church and Faith in the Patristic Tradition* (Aldershot: Variorum, 1996), No. V.

ry might have been spared a debate more characterized by zeal for the faith than by the sort of charity which is commonly taken for granted in modern ecumenical discussion.[34] It is possible to feel sorry for Pelagius. Far from being the proud heresiarch of tradition, he seems to have had little appetite for controversy and tried, so far as he could, to avoid it. He was caught up in a dispute over which he had no control.

No one who takes theological doctrines seriously will regard these issues of the Pelagian Controversy as unimportant. As Augustine repeatedly emphasized, underlying the debate on grace and free will were the major issues of the relation of the created being to its creator: the virtue of humility; man's place in God's creation. Following the mainstream of Christian tradition, Augustine held that God's omnipotence was a foundation assumption of Christian belief.[35] To this he added his conviction that baptism was essential for salvation and that the great majority of the human race would be damned. However distasteful such convictions may be to most Christians today, Augustine could claim the authority of Scripture; and behind all this was that text of St. Paul which had overwhelmed him in 397: *What have you that you did not receive? If then you received it why do you boast as if it were not a gift?* With such a foundation of thought it is not surprising that Augustine's predestinar-

34. In fairness to Augustine, he seems to have tried to do justice to Pelagius's intentions until alarmed for what he deemed to be Gospel truth—and perhaps for his own theological reputation—by misleading accounts of Pelagius's vindication at the Synod of Diospolis. There is also the possibility of simple misunderstanding of the other side's arguments. Columba Stewart's verdict on the opponents in the Messalian Controversy is worth remembering: "Had they lived in another age, with major research libraries, dictionaries, and concordances available to them, they might have worked it all out." *"Working the Earth of the Heart," The Messalian Controversy in History, Texts and Language to A.D. 431* (Oxford: Clarendon Press, 1991), 238.

35. See *De Fide et Symbolo* 2,2–3: "Sed qui praestat rebus formam, ipse praestat etiam posse formam. . . . Quapropter rectissime creditur omnia deum fecisse de nihilo . . . (3) Credentes itaque IN DEUM OMNIPOTENTEM, nullam creaturam esse, quae ab omnipotente non creata sit existimare debemus." *CSEL* 41,5–6; *De Symbolo ad Catechumenos* 2: "Nemo resistit omnipotenti, ut non quod vult faciat. Ipse fecit caelum et terram, mare et omnia quae in eis sunt. . . . Fecit et hominem ad imaginem et similitudinem suam in mente; ibi est enim imago dei. . . . Facti sumus humiles mortales, impleti sumus timoribus, erroribus, hoc merito peccati, cum quo merito et reatu nascitur omnis homo." *CCL* 46,186.

ian thinking, while it was forced by the text of the Bible to admit human freedom, made that freedom dependent upon an immediate impulse of grace, and emphasized human helplessness until grace comes. Yet in the practical business of pastoral relationships, Augustine was constrained to recognize human free choice as a reality, and this meant in practice to admit responsibility.

For Pelagians the intellectual problem was different. They were not an organized party like the African bishops but a fortuitous group, sharing a common outlook if not identical views. One might say that while accepting God's omnipotence as Creator, they regarded man as being endowed with free choice in his creation and retaining his freedom, even after sinning, though denying any transmission of Original Sin. For Augustine and his African colleagues, this was heresy. Whether by the standards of the fifth Christian century it was such is open to question—confession of Original Sin was not to be found in any ecumenical creed, and the Greek Fathers understood it as an inherited weakness rather than inherited guilt.[36] It is at least debatable whether the Pelagians refused to acknowledge assisting grace, as Augustine alleged.[37] What they did was to emphasize human responsibility by declaring that man has the power to act righteously in the present life. In a sense, they were prolonging an assumption of the pre-Constantinian Church: that the baptized Christian, with his sins remitted, is now a free agent; hence the harshness of the treatment of those who lapsed under the threat of persecution.[38] It required the mass apostasies of the Decian Persecution to persuade the

36. See Mozley, *Predestination*, 3rd ed., 105–6; N. P. Williams, *The Ideas of the Fall and of Original Sin* (London, 1927), 310–14. The observation of Vladimir Lossky, *The Mystical Theology of the Eastern Church* (English translation of a French original, London, 1957), 198: "The fundamental error of Pelagius was that of transposing the mystery of grace on to a rational plane, by which process grace and liberty, realities of the spiritual order, are transformed into two mutually exclusive concepts which then have to be reconciled," does not do Pelagianism justice.

37. See above, note 32.

38. The mood of conversion in some pre-Constantinian converts is vividly depicted by St. Cyprian in *Ad Donatum* 2–3. *CSEL* 3, 5–7. Cyprian seems to envisage a psychological, as well as a spiritual, rebirth in the baptized person, which should remove any possibility of serious sin.

Church to admit the possibility of penance and restoration to communion of the fallen. The Pelagians stood in this rigorist tradition, to which was added the influence of the appeal of asceticism popularized by the rise of monasticism, an asceticism which was commended by as orthodox a thinker as Jerome no less enthusiastically than by Pelagius.

In a study of Augustinian predestination first published in 1855,[39] J. B. Mozley, brother-in-law of John Henry Newman and later Canon of Christ Church, Oxford, and Regius Professor of Divinity, theologically orthodox but fair-minded and aware of the limitations of the human intellect, noted that the ideas of Divine Power and human free will, while sufficiently clear for the purposes of practical religion, are, in this world, truths from which we cannot derive definite and absolute systems. "All that we build upon either of them must partake of the imperfect nature of the premise which supports it, and be held under a reserve of consistency with a counter conclusion from the opposite truth."[40] The Pelagian and Augustinian systems both arise upon partial and exclusive bases. Mozley held that while both systems were at fault, the Augustinian offends in carrying certain religious ideas to an excess, whereas the Pelagian offends against the first principles of religion:[41] "Pelagianism . . . offends against the first principles of piety, and opposes the great religious instincts and ideas of mankind. It . . . tampers with the sense of sin"—a hard saying and one which conflicts with what Mozley says elsewhere.[42] It may be that Mozley, who had earlier questioned Augustine's denunciation of Pelagius's doctrine of grace as inadequate,[43] was unnecessarily hard in his judgment. The Pelagians, in particular Julian of Eclanum, did maintain certain notions of divine mercy and justice which Augustine's system set aside for explanation on the day of judgment; but Mozley's belief that Augustine's "doctrine of the Fall, the doctrine of Grace, and the doctrine of the Atonement are grounded in the instincts of mankind,"[44] is that of the Christian Church down the ages, if not of all humanity, and wit-

39. Mozley, *Predestination*, note 36 above.

40. Ibid., p. 27; cf. p. 305.

41. Ibid., p. 307.

42. Ibid., p. 308.

43. Ibid., p. 49, quoted in note 32 above.

44. Ibid., p. 309.

nessed by Augustine in the Christology which informs his thinking. It can only be regretted that he allowed the implications of this Christology to be limited by his conviction of the absolute character of divine power.

But why was this the case? How was it that Augustine, with his powerful and wide-ranging mind, was content to take so narrow a view of the divine purpose for the greater part of humanity? Various explanations can be offered: the outlook of the Church of his day—or what he took to be the outlook of the Church, and particularly his own African Church; the harshness of some language of Scripture and of the reported words of Christ Himself; Augustine's own conviction of the overriding power of the Divine Will, to which everything created must yield; and a sense of the mystery of creation, which is insoluble in this life, allied to an element of hardness in his temperament which seems oddly at variance with a genuine sensibility to love and friendship. But none of these alone, nor all of them together, would seem to supply an explanation of the mind of this man who had, by any standards, an unusually powerful, enquiring, and sympathetic intellect. A possible explanation may lie in Augustine's apologetic tendency, a willingness to take up an issue, often polemical, to deal with it, sometimes at very great length, and then to address himself to another, on occasion even working on several topics simultaneously. In doing this he covered a huge range of subjects; but he never addressed himself to the construction of a single, comprehensive system, a *summa theologiae augustinianae,* in which he might have tried to harmonize the various elements in the Christian revelation.[45] It may well be that this would have been impossible. Augustine was too busy, too much occupied in controversy, to make rather than to find time to address himself to such a project; but it is greatly to be regretted that he was never moved to do so.

45. The *Enchiridion* is an exposition on the beliefs of the Creed, a practical doctrinal handbook, but it is not a personal statement of Augustine. *The Confessions* is personal devotion and not exposition, while the *De Trinitate,* despite its range, is for our purposes too narrowly focused. None of these has the speculative character of Origen's *De Principiis,* which Augustine never sought or desired to emulate.

SELECT BIBLIOGRAPHY

1. Reference

The most convenient Augustinian reference work today for English readers is *Augustine through the Ages: An Encyclopedia,* ed. Allan D. Fitzgerald (Grand Rapids, Mich.: Eerdmans; Cambridge, U.K., 1999). Written in English by an Anglo-American team of scholars, it covers all Augustine's writings and the main aspects and incidents, with detailed articles on his letters and sermons.

The *Augustinus-Lexikon,* edited by Cornelius Mayer and an international editorial team (Basel: Schwartz and Company), has articles in German, English, and French, without benefit of translation. Massively learned, it began publication in 1986 and by 2004 had reached vol. 3, fasc. ¾: "Hieronymus–Institutio, institutem." It is likely that all its original contributors, and certainly the present writer, will be dead by the time the last entry—presumably Zosimus—appears.

2. Modern Studies

Allin, Thomas. *The Augustinian Revolution in Theology.* London, 1911.

Augustine, *Answer to the Pelagians (The Works of St. Augustine: A Translation for the 21st Century),* introduction, translation, and notes by Raymond J. Teske, I, 23–25. New York: New City Press, 1997–99.

Babcock, William. "Augustine's Interpretation of Romans (A.D. 394–396)." *Augustinian Studies* 10 (1979): 55–74.

———. "Sin and Punishment: The Early Augustinian Evil." In *Augustine: Presbyter factus sum,* ed. J. T. Lienhard, E. C. Muller, and R. J. Teske, 235–48. New York: Peter Lang, 1993.

Beatrice, Pier F. *Tradux Peccati: Alle fonti della dottrina agostiniana del peccato originale.* Studia Patristica Mediolansia 8. Milan, 1978.

Bevan, Edwyn. *Symbolism and Belief.* London, 1938. Fontana Library ed., 1963.

Bochet, Isabelle. *Augustin et le désir de Dieu.* Paris: Études Augustiniennes, 1982.

Bonner, Gerald. *Augustine and Modern Research on Pelagianism.* The Saint Augustine Lecture 1970. Villanova, Pa., 1972. Reprinted in *God's Decree and Man's Destiny.* London, 1987, no. XI.

———. "Augustine and Mysticism." In *Augustine: Mystic and Mystagogue,* ed. F. van Fleteren, J. C. Schnaubelt, and Joseph Reino. New York, 1994.

———. *Augustine of Hippo: Life and Controversies.* 3rd ed. London, 2002.

———. "Augustine's Thoughts on This World and Hope for the Next." *The Princeton Seminary Bulletin,* supplementary issue no. 3 (1994): 85–103.

———. "Augustine's Understanding of the Church as a Eucharistic Community." In *St. Augustine the Bishop: A Book of Essays,* ed. F. Lemoine and C. Kleinhanz, 39–63. New York and London: Garland Publishing, 1994.

———. "The Doctrine of Sacrifice: Augustine and the Latin Patristic Tradition." In *Sacrifice and Redemption: Durham Essays in Theology,* ed. S. W. Sykes, 101–17. Cambridge: Cambridge University Press, 1991. Reprinted in *Church and Faith in the Patristic Tradition.* Aldershot: Variorum, 1996, no. XI.

———. "Pelagianism Reconsidered." *Studia Patristica* 27 (1993): 237–41. Reprinted in *Church and Faith in the Patristic Tradition.* Aldershot: Variorum, 1996, no. V.

———. "*Perceperunt mercedem suam.* The Background and Theological Implications of *De civitate Dei* V,15." *Studia Patristica* 18, 4 (1990): 3–7.

———. "Rufinus of Syria and African Pelagianism." *Augustinian Studies* 1 (1970): 31–17. Reprinted in *God's Decree and Man's Destiny.* London, 1987, no. X.

———. "The Significance of Augustine's *De Gratia Novi Testamenti.*" *Augustiniana* (1990): 531–59. Reprinted in *Church and Faith in the Patristic Tradition.* Aldershot: Variorum, 1996, no. IV.

Bouton-Touloubic, Anne-Isabelle. *L'ordre caché: La notion d'ordre chez saint Augustin.* Paris: Études Augustiennes, 2005.

Brown, Peter R. L. *Augustine of Hippo: A Biography.* London, 1967; 2nd ed. Berkeley, Calif., 2002.

———. *The Body and Society: Men, Women and Sexual Renunciation in Early Christianity.* London, 1989.

———. "The Patrons of Pelagius: The Roman Aristocracy between East and West." *Journal of Theological Studies,* n.s., 21 (1970): 56–72.

———. *Religion and Society in the Age of Augustine.* London, 1972.

Burnaby, John. *Amor Dei: A Study of the Religion of St. Augustine.* London, 1938.

———. "The *'Retractations'* of St. Augustine: Self-criticism or Apologia?" *Augustinus Magister.* Congrès internationale augustinien, Paris, 21–24 September 1954. Vol. 1: 85–92.

Burnell, Peter. *The Augustinian Person.* Washington, D.C., 2005.

Burnett, Carole. "Dysfunction at Diospolis." *Augustinian Studies* 34 (2003): 153–73.

Burns, J. Patout. "Augustine's Role in the Imperial Action against Pelagius." *Journal of Theological Studies,* n.s., 30 (1979): 67–83.

Bury, J. B. *History of the Later Roman Empire,* vol. 1. London, 1923.

Butler, Cuthbert. *Western Mysticism.* 3rd ed. London, 1967.

Cary, Philip. *Augustine's Invention of the Inner Self: The Legacy of a Christian Platonist.* Oxford: Oxford University Press, 2000.

Cayré, F. *La contemplation augustinienne.* 2nd ed. Bruges/Paris, 1954.

Clark, Mary. *Augustine: Philosopher of Freedom.* New York, 1958.

Courcelle, Pierre. *Recherches sur les "Confessions" de saint Augustin.* Paris, 1968.

Evans, R. F. *Pelagius: Inquiries and Reappraisals.* New York, 1968.

Flasch, Kurt. *Augustin: Einführung in sein Denken.* Stuttgart, 1980.

Fontanier, J.-M. *La Beauté selon Saint Augustin.* Presses Universitaires de Rennes, 1998.

Frend, William H. C. *Saints and Sinners in the Early Church.* London, 1985.

Friedriksen, Paula. "Beyond the Body/Soul Dichotomy: Augustine on Paul against the Manichees and the Pelagians." *Recherches Augustiniennes* 23 (1988): 87–114.

———. "Paul and Augustine: Conversion Narratives, Orthodox Traditions, and the Retrospective Self." *Journal of Theological Studies* 37 (1986): 3–34.

Ghellinck, J. de. *Patristique et Moyen Age: Études d'histoire littéraire et doctrinale.* Tom. III: *Compléments à l'étude de la Patristique* (Brussels/Paris, 1948), Étude VIII: "Une édition patristique célèbre," 339–65.

Gilson, Étienne. *Introduction à l'étude de saint Augustin.* 4th ed. Paris, 1969.

Hanby, Michael. *Augustine and Modernity.* London/New York, 2003.

Harnack, Adolf von. *Lehrbuch der Dogmengeschichte.* Bd. 3, 6th ed. Tübingen, 1960.

Harrison, Carol. *Augustine: Christian Truth and Fractured Humanity.* Oxford: Oxford University Press, 2002.

———. *Beauty and Revelation in the Thought of St. Augustine.* Oxford: Oxford University Press, 1992.

Henry, Paul. *La Vision d'Ostie.* Paris, 1938; English trans., *The Path to Transcendence.* Pittsburgh, 1981.

Hombert, Pierre-Marie. *Gloria Gratiae: Se glorifier en Dieu, principe et fin de la théologie augustinienne de la grace.* Paris: Institut d'Études Augustiniennes, 1996.

Knox, Ronald. *Enthusiasm: A Chapter in the History of Religion.* Oxford, 1950.

Lacey, T. A. *Nature, Miracle and Sin: A Study of St. Augustine's Conception of the Natural Order.* London, 1916.

Lancel, Serge. *St. Augustine,* trans. Antonia Level. London: S.C.M. Press, 2002.

Lossky, Vladimir. *The Mystical Theology of the Eastern Church.* English trans., London, 1957.

Lössl, Josef. *Julian von Aeclanum: Studien zu seinem Leben, seinen Werk, seiner Lehre und ihrer Überlieferung.* Leiden, 2001.

Louth, Andrew. *The Origins of the Christian Mystical Tradition.* Oxford, 1981.

Markus, Robert A. "Pelagianism, Britain and the Continent." *Journal of Ecclesiastical History* 37 (1986): 191–204.

Marrou, Henri. "Les attaches orientales du Pélagianisme," Académie des Inscriptions & Belles-Lettres: Comptes Rendus des Séances de l'Année 1968, 459–72.

Masterson, Patrick. *Atheism and Alienation.* London: Pelican Books, 1973.

Merdinger, J. E. *Rome and the African Church in the Time of Augustine.* New Haven and London, 1997.

Mozley, J. K. *A Treatise on Augustinian Predestination.* 3rd ed. London, 1883.

Neusch, Marcel. *The Sources of Modern Atheism,* trans. M. J. O'Connell. New York/Ramsey, N.J., 1982.

Nock, A. D. *Sallustius: Concerning the Gods and the Universe.* Cambridge, 1936.

Nuvolone, F. G., and A. Solignac. "Pélage et Pélagianisme." *Dictionnaire de spiritualité, ascétique, mystique, doctrine et histoire* 12B (1986), 2889–942.

Nygren, Anders. *Agape and Eros,* trans. Philip S. Watson. London: SPCK, 1982.

O'Connell, Robert J. *Art and the Christian Intelligence in St. Augustine.* Oxford: Basil Blackwell, 1978.

Ó Cróinín, Dáibhí. "Who Was Palladius, 'First Bishop of the Irish'?" *Peritia* 15 (2001).

O'Donnell, James J. *Augustine: Sinner and Saint.* New York/London, 2005.

Ogliari, D. *Gratia et Certamen: The Relationship between Grace and Free Will in the Discussion of Augustine with the So-called Semipelagians.* Bibliotheca Ephemeridum Theologicarum Lovaniensium, 169. Louvain, 2003.

Patte, Daniel, and E. TeSelle. *Engaging Augustine on Romans.* Hamburg, Pa., 2002.

Prestige, G. L. *Fathers and Heretics: Six Studies in Dogmatic Faith.* London, 1958.

Rees, B. R. *The Letters of Pelagius and His Followers.* Woodbridge, 1991.

———. *Pelagius: A Reluctant Heretic.* Woodbridge, 1988.

Rist, John. *Augustine: Ancient Thought Baptized.* Cambridge: Cambridge University Press, 1994.

Ryan, John K. *The Confessions of St. Augustine.* New York, 1960.

Salamito, Jean-Marie. *Les virtuoses et la multitude. Aspects sociaux de la controverse entre Augustin et les pélagiens.* Grenoble: Editions Jérome Millon, 2005.

Sherwin White, A. N. *Roman Society and Roman Law in the New Testament.* Oxford, 1963.

Solignac, A. *See* Nuvolone, F. G.

Stewart, Columba. *Cassian the Monk.* New York/London, 1998.

TeSelle, Eugene. "Rufinus the Syrian, Caelestius, Pelagius: Explorations in Prehistory of the Pelagian Controversy." *Augustinian Studies* 3 (1972): 61–95.

Thier, Sebastian. *Die Kirche bei Pelagius.* Berlin/New York, 1999.

Thrower, James. "Atheism," in *The Oxford Companion to Christian Thought.* Oxford, 2000.

Trapè, Agostino. *Saint Augustine: Man, Pastor, Mystic,* trans. Matthew J. O'Connell. New York, 1986.

Weaver, Rebecca Hardin. *Divine Grace and Human Agency.* Macon, Ga., 1996.

Wetzel, James. "Snares of Truth: Augustine on Free Will and Predestination." In *Augustine and His Critics,* ed. Robert Dodaro and George Lawless, 124–41. London/New York, 2000.

Wickham, Lionel. "Pelagianism in the East." In *The Making of Orthodoxy: Essays in Honour of Henry Chadwick,* ed. Rowan Williams, 200–211. Cambridge, 1989.

Williams, N. P. *The Ideas of the Fall and of Original Sin.* London, 1927.

INDEX

Freedom and Necessity: St. Augustine's Teaching on Divine Power and Human Freedom was designed and typeset in Dante by Kachergis Book Design of Pittsboro, North Carolina. It was printed on 60-pound Natural Offset and bound by McNaughton & Gunn of Saline, Michigan.